PLEASE SORRY THANKS

PLEASE
SORRY
THANKS

The Three Words
That Change Everything

MARK BATTERSON

MULTNOMAH

To my mom and dad.
Thanks for teaching me to say please, sorry, and thanks!

Contents

Part 3:
The Theology of *Thanks*

Introduction

Abracadabra

In the beginning was the Word.
—John 1:1

According to linguists, *abracadabra* **is the most** universally used word that doesn't need translation.[1] It's a word employed by magicians, but the etymology is more spiritual than magical. The ancient words *A'bra K'dabra* mean "As I speak, I shall create."[2] In other words, words create worlds! "Words," said the Jewish theologian Abraham Heschel, "are themselves sacred, God's tool for creating the universe, and our tools for bringing holiness—or evil—into the world."[3]

In a series of studies conducted at the University of Chicago, the recordings of thousands of counseling sessions were analyzed. Some sessions were successful, resulting in sustained change. Others were unsuccessful. The differentiating factor? It wasn't the therapist's technique. "The difference," said Dr. Eugene Gendlin, "is in *how* [the counselees] talk."[4] Life is a grand game of Simon Says, and you're Simon!

If you want to change your life, you have to change your words!

Our words don't represent the world objectively. Rather, our words create the world subjectively! For better or for worse, our words can function as self-fulfilling prophecies. They have the power to bless or to curse, to heal or to hurt, to give life or to cause death. Scientific studies have found that negative words spoken to plants cause them to languish while positive words help them flourish.[5] It's as true of people as it is of plants!

"The tongue," said Solomon, "has the power of life and death."[6] The Jewish sage Akila the Translator "defined the tongue as a tool having a knife at one end and a spoon at the other"—death and life.[7] The tongue is a two-edged sword. "With the tongue we praise our Lord and Father," said James, the half brother of Jesus, "and with it we curse human beings, who have been made in God's likeness."[8] He likened the tongue to the rudder of a ship, which determines its direction.[9] Your destiny, to a large degree, is a derivative of your words.

"Out of the overflow of the heart," Jesus said, "the mouth speaks."[10] Words are like X-rays, but they do more than reveal the condition of our hearts. Our words are both a diagnosis and a prognosis. Dr. John Gottman is famous for his ability to predict divorce with more than 90 percent accuracy. How? He examines language in thin slices and analyzes the way people argue. In doing so, Dr. Gottman identified negative communication patterns that he called "the four horsemen of the apocalypse"—criticism, contempt, defensiveness, and stone-walling.[11]

If you want to change your relationships, you have to change your words.

Can I make a confession? The political polarization of recent years has taken a toll on my life and leadership. Low levels of civility coupled with high levels of cynicism have created the perfect storm.

It feels like no matter what you say, it's never enough and it's always too much. Or is that just me? You're damned if you do, damned if you don't. Positivity is one of my strengths, but I recently found myself in a funk. Here's a journal entry from one of those down days when I felt like I was emotionally flatlining:

I'm so spent.
I'm so tired.
It feels like I'm running on empty.
I'm just not bouncing back.
My head is foggy.
My heart is irritated.
Lord, help me.

I did a lot of self-examination during that season, and one revelation was that I was using negative words with a high degree of frequency. You know what I realized? I was speaking negativity into existence and giving it power. By emphasizing how hard leadership was during that season, I was making it harder than it had to be! My words became a self-fulfilling prophecy that reinforced a vicious cycle of negativity. The same thing happens when you complain about people behind their backs, which was a second revelation. Want to change that dynamic? You flip the script by catching people doing things right, then bragging about them behind their backs!

If you want to change your attitude, you have to change your words.

Your words are Occam's razor—simple words can solve

seemingly impossible problems. Your words are Archimedes's lever—small words can make a world of difference.

This book is about three small yet powerful words: *please, sorry,* and *thanks.* Often referred to as magic words, they can work wonders. Nothing opens doors like *please.* Nothing mends fences like *sorry.* Nothing builds bridges like *thanks.* These three words have the power to change your life. They have the power to change the lives of those who love you, those who hate you, and everyone in between.

In the pages that follow, we'll explore the psychology of *please,* the science of *sorry,* and the theology of *thanks.* Along the way, we'll learn the art of empathy. We'll cultivate emotional intelligence and contextual intelligence. And I'll cite stories and studies, along with some best practices, that will help you change your life by changing your words. But first, a word from our Sponsor, and I mean that literally. To understand the power of words, we must go back to the very beginning.

God said, "Let there be light."[12]

According to Leonard Bernstein, winner of seven Emmys and sixteen Grammys, a better translation than *said* is *sang.* "In the beginning was the note, and the note was with God," said the former conductor of the New York Philharmonic, "and whosoever can reach for that note, reach high, and bring it back to us on earth, to our earthly ears—he is a composer."[13]

On that note (pun intended), every atom in the universe sings a unique song. In more scientific terms, every atom emits and absorbs energy at a unique frequency. It's true of every element in the periodic table, it's true of you, and it's true of words. Life-giving words resonate with that original note.

Destructive words do the opposite. They cause internal dissonance because they are at odds with God's good, pleasing, and perfect will.

Few words resonate with more power than *please, sorry,* and *thanks.* They sing in three-part harmony. A pretty *please* opens hearts and minds and doors. A simple *sorry* can mend broken relationships. A heartfelt *thanks* is the flywheel of gratitude.

There is an art and science to all three words. We'll wordsmith *please, sorry,* and *thanks,* approaching them as an art form. But let me start with science. Whether God *said* or *sang* those first words—"Let there be light"—we tend to think in terms of phonics. But sound is, first and foremost, a form of energy. So, really, we should think physics. Our words don't just exchange ideas; they exchange energy.

The human voice produces sound waves that travel through space at 1,125 feet per second. The average female speaks at a frequency of 170–220 hertz. The average male, after puberty, speaks at a lower pitch of 100–150 hertz. Mariah Carey is famous for her five-octave range, but the rest of us have a vocal range between roughly 55 and 880 hertz.

We also have a range of hearing between 20 and 20,000 hertz. Anything below 20 hertz is infrasonic. Anything above 20,000 hertz is ultrasonic. This is when and where and how sound does strange and mysterious things. Infrasound is how elephants predict changes in weather and how birds navigate as they migrate. Ultrasound can be used to track submarines, guide noninvasive surgery, clean jewelry, heal damaged tissue, break up kidney stones, and reveal the gender of a baby via sonogram.

Does God speak audibly? Absolutely! But that's a thin slice of His vocal range. His ability to speak is way beyond our ability to hear. God doesn't just use His voice to form words; He uses words to form worlds! Everything we *see* was once *said*. Or, if you prefer, *sung*. God used His voice to create ex nihilo— *abracadabra*.

> In the beginning was the Word, and the Word was with God, and the Word was God. He was with God in the beginning. Through him all things were made; without him nothing was made that has been made.[14]

The Doppler effect tells us that the universe is still expanding. In other words, the words God spoke in the beginning are still creating galaxies at the outer edge of the universe. The universe is God's way of saying, "Look at what I can do with four words!" Everything we *see* was once *said*.

Most people claim that they have never heard the voice of God. If you're referring to the audible voice of God, no argument here. But there is a reality that goes way beyond what we can taste, touch, see, smell, or hear. God uses His infrasonic and ultrasonic voice to heal and to reveal, to guide and to gift, to convict and to create.

I know what you're thinking: *I can't speak things into existence.* Not so fast. You may not be able to big bang the universe, but like the God in whose image you were created, your words create worlds.

When we enter the world, our primary means of communication is crying. Give it a few months, and babies start forming their first syllables. The average toddler has somewhere between fifty and one hundred words in their vocabulary. When we're toddlers, words are the way we make sense of the world. Words are also the way we get our way! The same holds true for adults. Our vocabulary expands exponentially, as does our ability to communicate with tone and body posture, but we use words for the same reason.

The *Oxford English Dictionary* has an estimated 171,476 words in use in the English language, and there are an estimated 47,156 words that are now obsolete.[15] "According to lexicographer and dictionary expert Susie Dent, 'the average active vocabulary of an adult English speaker is around 20,000 words, while his passive vocabulary is around 40,000 words.' "[16]

I don't know whether your vocabulary is above average or below average, but I have a theory. You only need to be good at three things to be successful at whatever you do. What are those three things? Three words—*please, sorry,* and *thanks.* All right, maybe you won't succeed at Scrabble or the spelling bee. But you'll succeed at everything else.

If you want to be a doctor, I advise med school. If you want to be a lawyer, go to law school. But your degree isn't what will earn you promotions. Lots of people have PhDs. The best predictor of success in life, in love, and in leadership is your proficiency at *please, sorry,* and *thanks.*

"About 15 percent of one's financial success is due to one's technical knowledge," said Dale Carnegie, "and about 85 percent is due to skill in human engineering."[17] When it comes to human engineering, the high-leverage points are *please, sorry,* and *thanks!* Those three words are the foundation of all healthy relationships. Those three words are the only ceiling on your spiritual, mental, and emotional health. Those three words will determine how happy you are and, I might add, how holy you are.

How do you cultivate intimate relationships?

How do you make amends for the mistakes you've made?

How do you overcome trauma?

How do you find true happiness?

How do you shift the atmosphere at home?

How do you change the culture at work?

How do you win friends and influence people?

You get really good at *please, sorry,* and *thanks*! Of course, you can't just parrot those words. You have to walk the talk. Those three words have to become a way of life, a rule of life. Please hear me when I say, you can change the world. How? With your words. Words create worlds!

PLEASE SORRY THANKS

Part 1

THE PSYCHOLOGY
OF *PLEASE*

In 1879, Francis Galton invented the word-association test, "a test in which the participant responds to a stimulus word with the first word that comes to mind."[1] Carl Jung employed this test to survey the subconscious minds of his patients. Patients were prompted with one hundred stimulus words, and their responses revealed past trauma, subliminal fears, and internal conflicts. Jung paid particular attention to the words that caused a visceral reaction. There were trigger words that elicited negative emotions and painful memories, and there were words that did the exact opposite.[2] Like the balm of Gilead, words can have healing properties. Or words can ricochet around the mind with all the chaos of a pinball.

We each have a unique relationship with words. We hear them differently based on our experiences. When my son Josiah was a little boy, he thought the word *disciple* meant "storm." My best guess is that I was reading him the story about the storm that hit the disciples on the Sea of Galilee, and he must have conflated those meanings. When storm clouds would form in the sky, he used to say, "The disciples are coming." Right or wrong, different words mean different things to different people.

If I say *blue,* what comes to mind? For many of us, the automatic association is sky. If your work or interest lies in politics, you think blue states and red states. If you graduated from Michigan, you associate the word with Big Blue. Or maybe you grew up on *Blue's Clues* and now you're hearing the theme song in your head. Words conjure up age-old memories, evoke deep-seated emotions, put our defense mechanisms on red alert, and catalyze crazy ideas. And they do so without our conscious awareness.

For decades, a social psychologist named John Bargh has conducted studies on the way words affect behavior. In one such study, undergraduate students were given a scrambled-sentence test. One version of the test was sprinkled with rude words like *disturb, bother,* and *intrude.* Another version was sprinkled with polite words like *respect, considerate,* and *yield.* The subjects thought they were taking tests measuring language ability, but they were actually being subconsciously primed by those words.

Priming is a psychological phenomenon related to stimulus and response, and words are the lead actors. The word *nurse* is recognized more quickly if it's preceded by the word *doctor.* The same goes for *dog* and *wolf.* Why? These words are semantic primes that cause you to think in categories. If I say *Empire State Building,* it puts you in a New York state of mind. In the same sense, the word *please* is a politeness prime.

After taking the five-minute scrambled-sentence test, students were supposed to walk down the hall and talk to the person running the experiment about their next assignment. An actor was strategically engaged in conversation with the researcher when the students arrived. The goal? Bargh wanted to see whether the subjects who were primed with polite words would wait longer before interrupting than those who were primed with rude words. The result? Sixty-five percent of the group primed with rude words interrupted the conversation. Those primed with polite words? Eighty-two percent of them never interrupted at all.[3] If the test hadn't timed out at ten minutes, who knows how long they would have waited?

A few polite words. What difference do they make? In quantitative terms, they can make a 47 percent difference! Don't underestimate the power of polite words, especially the word *please*.

Please adds respect and urgency to a request. It's asking instead of demanding, but it's only as effective as it is authentic. If you try to use the word to manipulate, it will have the opposite effect. Our motives must match our words. You have to say what you mean and mean what you say!

For the love of Emily Post, we need a revival of politeness, and it starts with *please*. "It sets the tone for whatever follows and is one of the most important universal manners."[4] Nothing primes the pump like *please,* especially if you put a *pretty* in front of it. How does it work? "It changes a command into a request."[5] News flash: No one wants to be told what to do!

When Christian Herter was governor of Massachusetts, he stopped by a church barbecue after a long day on the campaign trail. As he made his way down the serving line, he asked whether he could have a second piece of chicken. The woman serving the chicken said, "Sorry. Only one to a customer." Governor Herter was a humble man, but he was also hungry. "Do you know who I am? I'm the governor of the state." Without skipping a beat, the woman replied, "Do you know who I am? I'm the lady in charge of the chicken. Move along, mister!"[6]

Demands come across as entitled, governor or not. A simple *please* levels the playing field. It will get you further than your title, your rank, or your credentials. Authenticity trumps authority, like a royal flush. The word *please* demonstrates a posture of humility, and no one did it better than Jesus.

> Do nothing out of selfish ambition or empty pride, but in humility consider others more important than yourselves. Each of you should look not only to your own interests, but also to the interests of others.

> Let this mind be in you which was also in Christ Jesus:

> Who, existing in the form of God,
>   did not consider equality with God
>   something to be grasped,
> but emptied Himself,
>   taking the form of a servant.[7]

Theologians call this kenosis, Christ's emptying of Himself for others. And we are called to do the same. It's all about adding value to others. You can learn the subtle art of persuasion, and it may help you get what you want. But all too often, persuasion is abused for selfish purposes. It turns into a zero-sum game. There is a better way, the Jesus way. It's giving yourself away. It's looking out for the interests of others. The locus of focus is others.

Please is setting aside your preferences.

Please is relinquishing your rights.

Please is giving others the upper hand.

Please is putting the ball in someone else's court.

Please is honoring others above yourself.

When you put a *please* in front of a request, it has a ripple effect. It's called the law of reciprocity. When someone is nice to you, you have an innate urge to be nice in return. The psychology of *please* isn't rocket science. It's as simple as the Golden Rule: "Treat people the same way you want them to treat you."[8] And it starts with *please*!

1

There *You* Are

It's not about you.
—RICK WARREN, *The Purpose Driven Life*

Jennie Jerome, Winston Churchill's mother, once dined with two of Britain's prime ministers on back-to-back evenings. When asked her impression of each, she said of William Gladstone, "When I left the dining room after sitting next to Gladstone, I thought he was the cleverest man in England." After dining with Benjamin Disraeli? "I left feeling that I was the cleverest woman."[1]

William Gladstone was good at projecting his charismatic personality, and there is nothing inherently wrong with that. We naturally want to put our best foot forward. Benjamin Disraeli was good at drawing water out of other people's wells. He brought the best out of others. The difference? Gladstone was self-focused, while Disraeli was others-focused. "Talk to people about themselves," said Disraeli, "and they will listen for hours."[2]

My spiritual father, Dick Foth, says there are two kinds of people in the world. The first kind of person walks into a room and internally announces, *Here I am*. They are pretty impressed with themselves. Their ego barely fits through the door. It's all about me, myself, and I. The second kind of person? They walk into a room and internally announce, *There you are*. They check their ego at the door. It's all about everyone else. Their objective is adding value.

Which one are you?

Are you a *here I am* person?

Or are you a *there you are* person?

People who try to impress others are unimpressive. What's really impressive is someone who isn't trying to impress anyone at all. In the same vein, the most interesting people are those who take a genuine interest in others. They ask lots of questions, and they follow up with "Tell me more!"

The famous apologist Francis Schaeffer said, "If I have only an hour with someone, I will spend the first 55 minutes asking questions and finding out what is troubling their heart and mind, and then in the last 5 minutes I will share something of the truth."[3] Schaeffer understood the virtue of listening. His wife, Edith, described him as having a ministry of conversation.[4]

Did you know that Teddy Roosevelt read, on average, a book a day? And that was while serving as president?[5] How did he do it? For starters, he wasn't watching TV or surfing social media! There were far fewer distractions a century ago, but I don't think he'd read any less if he were alive today. Why? Roosevelt had a holy curiosity about all of God's creation, and reading was his way of researching. Roosevelt prepared for guests, prepared for conversations, by doing his homework. What if we approached relationships, approached conversations, that way? We'd talk about the weather a whole lot less!

Are you living at a conversational pace? And when you have a conversation, do you do more talking or listening? I've had people fly across the country to spend an hour with me, and I couldn't get a word in edgewise. Trust me—I love hearing people's stories. But I was left wondering why they wanted to talk to me. I guess they literally wanted to talk!

Here's a thought: God gave us two ears and one mouth—use them in that proportion! What does that have to do with *please*? *Please,* like listening, is others-focused. It's asking for permission, which empowers the other party. It puts them in the captain's chair.

Author and professor Adam Grant made a distinction between *givers* and *takers*.[6] Takers have a scarcity mindset. They tend to be self-focused: *Here I am.* It's a dog-eat-dog world, and their primary interest is self-interest. Givers have an abundance mindset—what goes around comes around. Their objective is adding value to others: *There you are.*

Givers and takers have diametrically opposed metrics of success. For a taker, whoever has the most toys at the end of the game wins. It's all about getting what's theirs. A giver doesn't just love to give; they live to give. In the words of martyred missionary Jim Elliot, "He is no fool who gives what he cannot keep to gain that which he cannot lose."[7]

My friend Brad Formsma wrote *I Like Giving.* It's the gold standard when it comes to generosity. It's all about inspiring people to be generous with their thoughts, words, money, time, attention, belongings, and influence. It was Brad who introduced me to Stanley Tam, the founder of the United States Plastic Corporation. When I met Stanley, he was well into his nineties and had given more than $120 million to kingdom causes. Over dinner he said something I'll never forget: "God's shovel is bigger than ours." In other words, you can't outgive God. Then he said something else that was simple yet profound: "God can't reward Abraham yet, because his seed is still multiplying."

What if we viewed words the way we view money?

What if we saw our words as gifts?

What if we were generous with life-giving words?

"Whatever you did for one of the least of these brothers and sisters of mine," Jesus said, "you did for me."[8] This is the transitive property applied to generosity. You can't bless others without blessing God. Life-giving words are the gift that keeps on giving.

How do you know whether you're a giver or a taker? Your itemized deductions for charitable giving are a pretty good indicator, but the most significant clue may be pronouns. Yes, pronouns.

Pronouns—and other function words like articles and prepositions—"account for less than one-tenth of 1 percent of your vocabulary but make up almost 60 percent of the words you use."[9] Pronouns are little words, but they have subtle power. "Since takers tend to be self-absorbed," said Adam Grant, "they're more likely to use first-person singular pronouns like *I, me, mine, my,* and *myself*—versus first-person plural pronouns like *we, us, our, ours,* and *ourselves.*"[10] In a study of CEOs who were extreme takers, 39 percent of their first-person pronouns were singular.[11]

There is a fascinating branch of psychology that analyzes word usage to gain psychological insight. Professor James Pennebaker created a software program called Linguistic Inquiry and Word Count, and he has used it to analyze everything from song lyrics to terrorist correspondence. The FBI asked Pennebaker to study al-Qaeda's communications—letters, videos, interviews. He discovered that Osama bin Laden's use of personal pronouns like *I, me,* and *mine* stayed close to baseline over time. But he saw a dramatic spike in the use of those words by bin Laden's second-in-command, Ayman al-Zawahiri. "This dramatic increase," said Pennebaker, "suggests greater insecurity, feelings of threat, and perhaps a shift in his relationship with bin Laden."[12]

In the world of politics, there are two primary ways to rally the troops. First, you can focus on a *common enemy* and demonize those who dare disagree with you. This approach is incredibly effective if your goal is inciting negative emotions such as fear, hate, and anger. It may win some votes, but it further divides people into *me versus you*. Rabbi Jonathan Sacks calls it pathological dualism—it prejudges people as "unimpeachably good" and "irredeemably bad."[13] The reality? "The line dividing good and evil," said Alexander Solzhenitsyn, "cuts through the heart of every human being." The common enemy approach is a zero-sum game.

The second way is to celebrate our *common humanity*—the image of God in me greets the image of God in you. It levels the playing field by humanizing one another. Few people were more effective than Dr. Martin Luther King, Jr., who appealed to common values, common ideals, and common sense. "Hate cannot drive out hate," said Dr. King, "only love can do that." What is your bent—*common enemy* or *common humanity*?

These two approaches lead to very different destinations, and pronouns are where the road divides. Instead of *me versus you*, a common-identity approach turns *me* into *we*.

As a leader, I pay close attention to pronouns. If I'm using a lot of first-person singular pronouns, it may indicate that I'm leading from a place of insecurity. I'm too focused on protecting my ego. I want more credit than I deserve. We flip that script by using plural pronouns that make it about we, not me. "It is amazing what you can accomplish," said President Harry Truman, "if you don't care who gets the credit."

When testosterone levels go up, our use of social pronouns—*we, us, they, them*—goes down.[14] Why? We become more task-oriented and less relationship-oriented, which often means that relationships are sacrificed for the sake of the goal. It's my way or the highway. Get on the bus or get run over by it.

Are you a *me* person?

Or are you a *we* person?

Self-centered leaders take the credit and shift the blame.

Others-focused leaders give the credit and take the blame.

King Saul is an excellent case study in insecurity. At the outset of his administration, he experienced a measure of success. His response? "Saul built an altar to the LORD."[15] So far, so God. Saul was giving credit where credit was due. But less than one chapter later, it says, "Saul went to the town of Carmel to set up a monument to himself."[16]

Those two verses recount defining moments, and they reveal a tragic flaw in Saul's character. If you find your identity in Christ, you build altars to God. If you're trying to prove yourself to people, you build monuments to yourself. And the more insecure you are, the bigger those monuments have to be! Remember Nebuchadnezzar? He built a ninety-foot statue to himself and demanded that people bow down before it.[17] Who does that? Someone who is compensating for an awful lot of insecurity!

Are you building altars to God?

Or are you building monuments to yourself?

During the days of King Saul, the Israelites sang a song that got Saul's goat: "Saul has slain his thousands, and David his tens of thousands."[18] Every time that song played on Spotify, it provoked a spirit of jealousy in Saul. "They credit David with ten thousands and me with only thousands," he said. "Next they'll be making him their king!"[19] What did Saul do? "From that time on Saul kept a jealous eye on David."[20]

Jealousy is one of the seven deadly sins. According to one theologian, it's "sorrow for another's good."[21] My favorite definition belongs to Robert Madu: "Jealousy is the trophy that mediocrity gives to excellence."[22] The only way to overcome jealousy, in my experience, is to do the opposite of what you feel. If you feel jealousy toward someone, brag about them behind their back. Better yet, compliment them to their face. Slowly but surely, it will defuse the jealousy. Until you can celebrate someone else's success, you aren't ready to experience success yourself.

The irony of the story? David was actually Saul's greatest asset. He helped Saul save face against Goliath—and saved Saul's kingdom. The beginning of the end? Saul started playing the comparison game, and no one wins the comparison game. The outcome is pride or jealousy, so either way, you lose!

What does any of this have to do with *please*?

Please is a first-person plural approach to life. It turns *me* into *we*. It's a win-win approach to relationships. "Win/Win is a belief in the Third Alternative," said Stephen Covey. "It's not your way or my way; it's a *better* way, a higher way."[23] I might add, the Jesus way. I live by a simple maxim: *If it's not a win for you, it's not a win for me.* The greatest of all is the servant of all. Instead of calling shotgun and taking the seat of honor, take the lowest seat at the table. Even if you're entitled to something, say please!

Even though I'm the lead pastor, I never use first-person singular pronouns when talking about National Community Church. Why? It's not *mine.* In some ways, NCC feels like a fourth child. We've invested a quarter century of blood, sweat, and tears, but I never call it *my* church. Why? Every pastor is an interim pastor. Every pastor is an undershepherd.

Jesus didn't say, "I will build *your* church." He didn't say, "*You* will build my church." He said, "I will build my church"—emphasis on *I* and *my*. It may seem like a small thing, but pronouns reveal whether leaders are self-focused or others-focused.

Pronouns reveal how sanctified or unsanctified our egos are.

Pronouns reveal whether we're givers or takers.

Pronouns reveal whether we're building altars to God or monuments to self.

Pronouns are the rudders that determine our destiny. They reveal where we find our identity. They reveal where we find our security. They even reveal idolatry!

The psychology of *please* starts with first-person plural pronouns. *We* is greater than *me.*

The power of *please* lives in the second person.

There *you* are!

2

Open Sesame

[Work] is the open sesame to every portal.
—WILLIAM OSLER

In 1964, Sidney Poitier became the first Black person to win an Academy Award for Best Actor. Not only did Poitier redefine roles for Black and African American actors and actresses by rejecting racial stereotypes; he did so with a smile. "He . . . opened doors for all of us that had been closed for years," said Denzel Washington.[1] Sidney Poitier used his influence to open doors, but what opened doors for Sir Sidney? Yes, he was knighted by Queen Elizabeth II in 1974. But long before that, Poitier's mother taught him to always say please and thank you. He took that instruction to heart and later said, "It was remarkable how many times *thank you* and *please* opened doors for me."[2]

For every success story, there is a backstory. "If you succeed without suffering, someone else did," said Joel Schmidgall. "If you suffer without succeeding, someone else will." The genealogy of success includes people the world will never know about, but you wouldn't be who you are without them. Their sacrifices set up your success.

King David didn't assume the throne without his thirty-seven mighty men. The apostle Paul didn't complete three missionary journeys without the twenty-nine friends who got honorable mentions in Romans 16—a first-century shout-out. Even Jesus didn't do what He did without His twelve disciples or the group of women who formed a hedge fund to support Him financially.

Author and pastor Eugene Peterson had three pictures that hung on the wall in his study. The first was John Henry Newman, who inspired his philosophy of ministry. The second was Baron Friedrich von Hügel, who influenced his love of language. The third was a Scottish preacher, Alexander Whyte. Every Sunday morning for more than twenty years, Peterson would read an Alexander Whyte sermon before preaching his own.

Those three luminaries served as watchmen on the wall. "They watched him as he studied and read," said his biographer, Winn Collier. "They watched as he labored over words to deliver, in prayer and from the pulpit."[3] Again, every success story has a backstory! There are people who are looking over our shoulders, people on whose shoulders we stand.

Along with those portraits, Eugene Peterson had a standing meeting on his calendar with "FD" three afternoons a week. Those initials stood for "Fyodor Dostoevsky." During a difficult stretch of leadership, Peterson read Dostoevsky's entire corpus. "Thanks to Dostoevsky," he said, "God and passion would never again be at risk."[4]

Who is your cloud of witnesses?

Whose portraits hang on the walls of your soul?

Who believed in you when you doubted yourself?

When Sidney Poitier was a teenager, he auditioned for an acting role at the prestigious American Negro Theatre in Harlem. He didn't get the part because he couldn't read the script. So Poitier started working as a dishwasher. One day an elderly Jewish waiter saw Poitier with a newspaper and asked him, "What's new in the paper?" Poitier said, "I can't tell you what's in the paper, because I can't read very well."[5]

After many weeks of this man's patient mentoring, Poitier learned to read well enough to land an apprentice role at the American Negro Theatre. When he received the Lifetime Achievement Award from the American Film Institute half a century later, he said, "I must also pay thanks to an elderly Jewish waiter who took time to help a young Black dishwasher learn to read."[6] Poitier paid tribute with the ultimate compliment: "A little bit of him is in everything I do."[7]

Legacy is not what you accomplish. Legacy is what others accomplish because of you. It's growing fruit on other people's trees, and it often starts with *please, sorry,* or *thanks!* It's being bold enough to offer help. It's being humble enough to accept help. Those are the moments that turn into tipping points.

William Osler, the father of modern medicine, said, "[*Work*] is the open sesame of every portal."[8] And I don't disagree. You have to work like it depends on you. But words matter too, and nothing says "Open sesame" like *please*!

Remember the story of Ali Baba and the forty thieves from *The Thousand and One Nights*? *Open sesame* is the phrase that opens the mouth of the cave in which is found hidden treasure. Nothing is better at opening impossible doors than a simple *please*.

All too often, we huff and puff and try to knock doors down

by exercising position or privilege. Why? We want the world to bow down to our every whim. We want the world to revolve around our every wish. So we use our titles as battering rams. Even God doesn't do that. Jesus is a gentleman!

Behold, I stand at the door and knock.[9]

In 1853, the English artist William Holman Hunt finished painting a portrait of Jesus standing at a door and knocking. It is a visual representation of this verse, and there is one feature that catches the eye. The door has no handle on the outside! Why? It must be opened from the inside. God has given us free will, and He will not violate it.

Are you knocking on doors?

Or are you knocking them down?

An old saying reminds us, *A man convinced against his will is of the same opinion still.* Our attempts to change people's opinions are usually met with resistance. It's like the old Aesop fable where the sun and the wind argued over who was stronger. The issue was settled with the help of an unsuspecting traveler who was wearing a cloak. Which one could make him disrobe? The wind began to blow, but the man clutched his cloak even more closely. Then the sun began to shine, and sure enough, a little bit of warmth caused the man to take off his cloak willingly.[10]

A *pretty please* is like a ray of sunlight. It's far more effective than trying to get your way through brute force. Not only does it win friends; it also wins enemies and turns them into friends. Persuasion is like the art of inception. You politely plant a seed in people's minds. How? Instead of issuing decrees, you ask questions. Instead of making demands, you make requests. *Please* gives people margin to own the idea, alter the idea, implement the idea. If they own the idea, it will own them. If they don't own it, you'll be doing a lot more managing than you want.

Can I make a confession? I'm a control freak! It's awfully hard to "let go and let God." But playing God is absolutely exhausting, and I'm not very good at it. So I've learned to give an extra measure of grace to people who have different experiences and personalities.

Be completely humble and gentle; be patient, bearing with one another in love.[11]

The last phrase can be translated this way: "tolerating one another in love." Tolerance doesn't mean relativism. That's a slippery slope. It's not a stamp of approval on anything that is outside God's good, pleasing, and perfect will. What is it? Biblical tolerance is giving other people the same measure of free will that God gives us. It's against my religion to impose my religion on anyone else! Oswald Chambers said it best: "Let God be as original with others as he is with you."

When you threaten people, they become defensive. The same goes for nagging. The more you push, the more they resist. Instead of trying to strong-arm people with gale-force winds, we should shine like stars. Isn't that what God does? When God wants us to change, He shows us kindness.[12] If that doesn't work? He shows us more kindness! It's reverse psychology—or maybe I should say, reverse theology. In the words of Selena Gomez, you "kill 'em with kindness."[13]

The Sermon on the Mount revolves around six counterintuitive instructions. We love our enemies, pray for those who persecute us, and bless those who curse us. We turn the other cheek, go the extra mile, and give the shirts off our backs. Those actions may be counterintuitive, but that's how we shift the atmosphere. That's how we operate in the opposite spirit. And when we do, it raises questions for which the gospel is the answer!

What does that have to do with the psychology of *please*? Nothing defuses defense mechanisms like a *pretty please*. *Please* is our Trojan horse. Instead of knocking down doors with a battering ram, we ask, seek, and knock.

> Ask and it will be given to you; seek and you will find; knock and the door will be opened to you.[14]

Those are present imperative verbs. In other words, you never arrive! You keep asking, keep seeking, keep knocking. No, not like a spammer who keeps calling your cell phone number. But I'll let you in on a little secret: *Bold prayers honor God, and God honors bold prayers.* Why? Bold prayers reveal big faith.

Let me make a distinction between two kinds of confidence. The locus of self-confidence is, you guessed it, self. The locus of holy confidence is the character of God. Even when we can't see His hand, we trust His heart. We know that God will withhold no good thing from those who walk uprightly before Him.[15]

> Which of you, if your son asks for bread, will give him a stone? Of if he asks for a fish, will give him a snake? If you, then, though you are evil, know how to give good gifts to your children, how much more will your Father in heaven give good gifts to those who ask him![16]

One of my favorite Christmas stories is about a little boy named Benjamin who wanted a baby sister for Christmas. He decided to write God a letter: "Dear God, I've been a very good boy . . ." He stopped writing, knowing it wasn't altogether true. "Dear God, I've been a pretty good boy . . ." That wasn't very convincing, so he wadded up the paper and threw it away. Benjamin decided on a different tack. He took the figurine of Mary from the family nativity underneath the Christmas tree and hid her under his bed. Then he rewrote his letter: "Dear God, if You ever want to see Your mother again . . ."

We chuckle at the naïveté, but we do the same thing, don't we? We aren't that overt, but we employ the same tactics—bribery and blackmail. *Dear God, if You do this, I'll do that. If You don't do this, I won't do that.* The good news? God has blessings for us in categories that we can't even conceive of. Of course, we have to posture ourselves for blessing. How? *Please* is a good place to start.

God won't answer 100 percent of the prayers you don't pray! You have not because you ask not.[17]

God is honored by our asking, but we have to ask for the right reasons. One word of caution: Some people are so busy climbing the ladder of success that they fail to realize it's leaning against the wrong wall. My advice? Don't seek opportunity. Seek God, and opportunity will seek you!

Open sesame!

3
Say It with a Smile

Smile; it's free therapy.
—DOUGLAS HORTON

Joey Reiman is the founder of BrightHouse, an ideation corporation that sells their ideas for millions of dollars. In his book *Thinking for a Living,* he shared about a rather unique sales pitch. There was stiff competition for an advertising account that he really wanted, and he got a tip. He knew the executives of that company were eating at Casa Mia, an upscale restaurant in Dallas. Joey Reiman paid off the maître d' and hired a mariachi band to sing his sales pitch. Needless to say, he got the contract.[1] But his best sales pitch may have been how he proposed to his girlfriend, Cynthia Good.

Cynthia was a news anchor, so Joey orchestrated a plan that involved the mayor of Atlanta, the police department, and the Japanese firm that owned the tallest building in Atlanta. Prior to the six o'clock news, the news director told Cynthia that a white-collar drug bust was about to happen in the penthouse of the IBM Tower and that the police chief was giving her the exclusive. She raced downtown with her camera crew, where she found twenty police cruisers and a SWAT team awaiting her arrival. The SWAT team escorted Cynthia to the fiftieth floor and broke down the door. But instead of a drug cartel, Joey Reiman dropped to one knee and proposed. She said yes! Then they enjoyed a dinner for two while watching the sun set over the city of Atlanta.[2]

If you're planning on getting engaged, no pressure!

Asking is an art form, isn't it? When done right, it involves thoughtful consideration. My advice? Pray it before you say it. The right word at the wrong time won't work. Timing is critical, and so is tone. When I record audiobooks, I try to smile. In one sense, that makes no sense because it's an *audio*book. But a smile changes the tone of your voice.

While we're on the subject, the science behind smiling is quite fascinating. Estimates vary, but some say it takes twenty-two facial muscles to smile, while it takes thirty-seven facial muscles to frown.[3] Save yourself some energy, and smile. Smiling relieves stress, boosts your immune system, reduces blood pressure, and helps you live longer. But wait—there's more. Smiling helps you stay positive and project confidence.[4]

When our kids were young, we had a mantra: *Your face tells your body how to feel.* You can shift your feelings with facial expressions. All you have to do is turn that frown upside down!

Studies indicate that children smile approximately 400 times per day while adults smile, on average, 20 times per day. Somewhere between childhood and adulthood, we lose 380 smiles per day. We've got to get some of those smiles back! That's part of what it means to become like little children. Smiling is the way we steward our forty-two facial muscles as well as the seventh cranial nerve that controls them. Fun fact? Smiling is scientifically proven to make you more attractive![5]

A smile adds *pretty* to *please!*

In the book of Daniel, the turning point is a bold ask. Daniel is punching above his weight.

Please test us for ten days on a diet of vegetables and water.[6]

I can't prove that Daniel said it with a smile, and I have no idea what tone of voice he used, but Daniel said please. He had tact, times ten.[7] His intelligence quotient had to be pretty high. After all, he spent three years studying the literature and language of the Babylonians. But I don't think that is what got him promoted to prime minister. The genealogy of success traces back to a simple *please*. It was a ten-day fast that set Daniel apart. He found favor, thanks to *please*.

According to Daniel Goleman, "At best, IQ contributes about 20 percent to the factors that determine life success." The other 80 percent is dependent on emotional intelligence.[8] Emotional intelligence is expressed through a wide range of abilities, which include motivating oneself, being persistent in the face of opposition, controlling emotional impulses, and regulating mood. The quintessence of emotional intelligence is empathy, which we'll explore in the section on the science of *sorry*.

One dimension of emotional intelligence is reading the room. It's not just saying what needs to be said. It's knowing when and how to say it. Daniel spoke "with wisdom and tact."[9] The Hebrew word for "tact" means "taste." Like a sommelier who can taste the tannins, the barrel, and the altitude and age of the grape, Daniel exercised discernment and operated with diplomacy. Tact is seeing past the presenting problem and identifying the root cause. It's understanding the ecosystem by connecting the dots.

Please must be spoken in a language that people can understand. On occasion, while eating at an Ethiopian restaurant, I'll say "Ameseginalehu." It's Amharic for "thank you." When I say it, those who speak Amharic light up. Why? I'm giving thanks in their language. Part of saying please is understanding the personality of the person you're talking to. What is their Enneagram number? What is their love language? You've got to say please in a language they understand and appreciate!

Let me get painfully practical. There are three keys to an effective *please,* and having only two out of three won't get you where you want to go. You need all three.

Your *Please* Has to Be Precise

You can't say please expecting carte blanche. Generally speaking, people don't write blank checks! Your *please* has to be well defined, like your words. The more nuanced it is, the more meaningful it is.

In her book *Caring for Words in a Culture of Lies,* Marilyn McEntyre said, "Stewardship of words is a high calling."[10] That's especially true of *please, sorry,* and *thanks.* McEntyre shared an assignment she gave a group of students where she asked them to write down their definitions of five words: *liberal, conservative, patriotic, terrorist,* and *Christian.* "The results were sobering," she said, "in their range and banality."[11] Why? If we can't agree on definitions, how do we dialogue? Imprecise words cause a great deal of polarization in the public sphere. Of course, the opposite is true as well. "If your verbs are precise," said McEntyre, "your writing will improve."[12] The same could be said for *please:* If your *please* is precise, your results will improve!

Notice how precise Daniel's *please* was. He specified their diet: vegetables. He defined the timeline: ten days. Your *please* has to define who, what, when, where, and why. People have a hard time saying yes if they don't know what they're saying yes to!

Remember the encounter Jesus had with a blind man named Bartimaeus? Jesus said, "What do you want me to do for you?"[13] That seems unnecessary, doesn't it? The answer is obvious—he wanted his sight restored. So why did Jesus ask? For starters, most of us don't know what we want. If Jesus asked us this question point-blank, many of us would draw a blank! Until you can precisely explain what you want and why you want it, you aren't ready for it.

There is one last lesson in this encounter. Quit putting words in people's mouths! Even Jesus didn't do that. There is a genius to what Jesus did here. He made the man say what he wanted in his own words. When we say what we want in our own words, we own it. It's called the generation effect in psychology. We have a better memory for things we've said out loud, things we've written down.

Your *Please* Has to Be Timely

"It is wonderful," said the writer of Proverbs, "to say the right thing at the right time!"[14] If your timing is off, it doesn't matter what you say! "If one blesses his neighbor with a loud voice early in the morning, it will be counted to him as a curse."[15]

During a very vulnerable season in my life, I was at an altar praying when a pastor put his hand on my shoulder and prayed for me. At some point during that prayer, it turned prophetic: "God is going to use you in a great way." Those ten words changed the trajectory of my life. Just as Sidney Poitier was indebted to the Jewish waiter who taught him to read, I owe that pastor a debt of gratitude. How do I pay him back? I exercise my own prophetic gifting to speak life-giving words to others!

What is the difference between a word of encouragement and a word of prophecy? A word of prophecy is inspired by the Holy Spirit, and it's often delivered at the moment when someone needs it most. The more precise, the more powerful.

As an author, I see the author in others. Sometimes it takes one to know one! Occasionally, I'll see a book in someone and I'll call it out. My friend Carey Nieuwhof inspires millions of leaders with his podcast. Carey recently released a brilliant book, *At Your Best*. I read the book all the way to the acknowledgments at the end, and I have to admit, I was a little surprised to see my name. Carey was kind enough to say this: "The first iteration of the concepts that became this book happened in 2015 when I spoke in Washington, DC, to Mark Batterson's staff." I remember that moment well. I said to Carey in no uncertain terms, "Please tell me that is going to be your next book!" Few things are more powerful than a prophetic *please,* a *please* spoken by the prompting of the Holy Spirit.

Your *Please* Has to Be Personal

When my father- and mother-in-law, Bob and Karen Schmidgall, were church planting in 1967, their denominational district superintendent and his wife paid a visit. Their original core group consisted of college students, so they were living on a diet of hot dogs, potato chips, and Kool-Aid. On the way out of town, E. M. and Estelle Clark stopped by the grocery store and bought steaks, baked potatoes, and ice cream for the entire team. A few days later, my mother-in-law received a gift in the mail—an electric knife, which she still uses and treasures more than fifty years later!

Have you ever been on the receiving end of an incredibly thoughtful gift? You never forget it, do you? Tim Delina is the senior pastor of Times Square Church in New York City. When Lora was going through a bout with cancer, Tim and his wife, Cindy, gave her a bracelet she has worn every day since. And they didn't just give her a bracelet; they put her on their prayer list. Many months later, Tim said, "We've prayed for Lora every single day!"

Your *please* is only as powerful as it is personal. You have to infuse it with your personality. You have to make your *please* a unique expression of who you are.

Many years ago, I accepted an invitation to speak at a conference for youth pastors. Honestly, it was a little outside my wheelhouse because I'd never been a youth pastor. Why did I say yes? The organizer sent me a life-size cardboard cutout of me! How could I say no to that? A little extra effort goes a long way these days, does it not? Generic requests are a dime a dozen. A personal *please* is tough to ignore! The more personal, the more memorable.

My friend Jarvis Glanzer pastors a church in the great state of Minnesota. I was born in Minneapolis, and our family vacationed at Lake Ida near Alexandria, Minnesota, when I was growing up. It was there, at nineteen years of age, that I felt called to ministry. I was taking a prayer walk through a cow pasture when I heard the inaudible yet unmistakable voice of God. That cow pasture is holy ground. I'm not sure what inspired this act of generosity, but Jarvis commissioned a piece of art. It's a map of Lake Ida etched into wood with the latitude and longitude of where I felt called to ministry. Few gifts are more meaningful, because few gifts are more personal.

All of us are creative! How do I know this? I've never met anyone who isn't creative when it comes to making excuses. That's called unsanctified creativity! What if we leveraged our creativity when it comes to *please, sorry,* and *thanks*? The world would be a much better place!

"Tell all the Truth," said Emily Dickinson, "but tell it slant."[16] My advice? Say please, but say it slant. Give it your unique signature by making it personal.

4

Wash Feet

Treat a man as he is, and he will remain as he is.
Treat a man as he can and should be, and he will
become as he can and should be.
—adapted from JOHANN WOLFGANG VON GOETHE,
Wilhelm Meister's Apprenticeship

As we age, the way we orient ourselves to the world changes. Until the age of twelve, most of us feel quite positive about ourselves. During our teen years, our self-esteem drops to its lowest levels. Not shocking, I know! Along with internal changes, the external peer pressure is almost unbearable. Teens feel the impossible desire to stand out and fit in at the same time. And social media isn't making it any easier. The good news? Our self-esteem gradually increases until the age of seventy! Most of us feel as good about ourselves at sixty-five as we did at nine years old.[1]

What does that have to do with the psychology of *please*? How you treat others is a function of how you feel about yourself. Hurt people hurt people by projecting their pain. They criticize in others what they don't like about themselves.

There is a third dimension to the Great Commandment that

is overlooked and underappreciated. We get the *love God* part. Same with *love your neighbor*. But notice the nuance: "Love your neighbor as yourself." If you don't like yourself, it's hard to love others! And when I say "like," I don't mean "likes" on social media.

Former Facebook employee Frances Haugen made headlines by testifying before a United States Senate committee on the negative impact of social media. Thirty-two percent of teen girls who feel bad about their bodies said that Instagram made them feel worse.[2] Is it any wonder? When our feeds are filled with filtered pictures of superfit people doing amazing things in exotic locations, we do a subconscious comparison. All of a sudden, we don't feel as good about what we see in the mirror. It's called upward counterfactual thinking.

The tendency to negatively compare ourselves with others never goes away, but it is an epidemic among teenagers. "Every time I feel good about myself," said one teen, "I go over to Instagram, and then it all goes away."[3]

According to a recent survey, 64 percent of Americans believe that social media is having a negative impact on our country.[4] This isn't shocking, is it? It's been said that we shape our tools and then our tools shape us. In the case of social media, distance demonizes. We say things online that we'd never say in person. We'd probably get punched if we did!

If social media has such a negative impact on us, why do we spend so much time and energy consuming its content? The answer is a phenomenon called doomscrolling. It's an ever-increasing appetite for doom and gloom. Like moths drawn to a flame, we're psychologically drawn to negative news. Did you know that 90 percent of all news stories are negative?[5] Headlines that use negative words like *bad* or *worst* are 30 percent

more effective at arresting attention than headlines with positive words. And the click-through rate is more than 60 percent
higher.[6] That negativity bias is a bigger deal than we realize. It
was a negative news report that kept Israel out of the Promised
Land. Ten negative people set a nation back forty years!

I'm not advocating Pollyanna positivity. We need a negative
feedback loop to *survive*. Without it, we keep making the same
mistakes over and over again. But we need a positive feedback
loop to *thrive*. Simply put, celebrate what you want to see more
of. Paul promoted this approach in his letter to the Ephesians:

> Don't use foul or abusive language. Let everything you say
> be good and helpful, so that your words will be an encour-
> agement to those who hear them.[7]

This rule of thumb applies whether you're talking or texting,
whether you're in person or online: *Don't say anything about anyone that you wouldn't say to their face.* I know that's easier said
than done, but that's the point of Paul's exhortation. The problem with social media is that it creates false anonymity.

At the risk of sounding like a Luddite, I'm profoundly concerned about the unintended consequences of social media.
For starters, I don't think we were designed to know everything
about everything in real time. It's like eating from the tree of
the knowledge of good and evil. What makes us think we can
ingest endless amounts of unfiltered media and not feel the effect? And then there are those who *post* about something on
social media and think they've also *done* something about it.
More often than not, it's just virtue signaling.

Half a century ago, a communications professor named

George Gerbner coined a term to describe a cognitive bias: *mean-world syndrome*.[8] If you're exposed to lots of violence-related content on television, you perceive the world as more dangerous than it really is.[9] Can I share some good news? I don't think people are as mean as they seem on social media. Of course, that doesn't excuse the trolling, baiting, bullying, and shaming. If social media is having a negative effect on you, muster the courage to quit. Or at least unfollow the people who feed the negativity.

Can I ask an honest question? What percentage of your thoughts, words, and actions is a regurgitation of the social media you consume? And what percentage of your thoughts, words, and actions is a revelation you're getting from God's Word?

Remember the old acronym GIGO? Garbage in, garbage out. It makes common sense, but let's be honest—most of us act like we're the exception to the rule. We think we can eat terribly and not feel the effect. We think we can get five hours of sleep and function at full capacity. We think we can leave our Bible on the shelf and still hear the voice of God. News flash: You are not an anomaly. You are what you eat. You are what you read. You are what you watch. I could keep going, but we'll stop there!

All too often, social media is anti-social. It has changed the tone of culture. We are more polarized and more politicized because of it. Politeness feels like an endangered species! The good news? That landscape makes your *please* all the more powerful.

Please is the way we level the playing field and find common ground.

Please is the way we show respect, even to those we disagree with.

Please is the way we bring some civility back to the public square.

I don't remember many of my dreams, but I had one a few years ago that was unforgettable. It was super succinct. In my dream, I was watching the trial of Jesus unfold. Pilate knew Jesus was innocent of the accusations being leveled against Him, but Pilate was afraid of popular opinion, so he tried to absolve himself of guilt by washing his hands. The problem with that is this: *Inaction* is an action, and *indecision* is a decision. It was a sin of silence. As Pilate washed his hands, I heard a voice say, "Don't wash your hands like Pilate; wash feet like Jesus." That's when I woke up!

Washing feet was the job reserved for the lowest-ranking servant, but that didn't keep Jesus from doing just that. He took responsibility for something that wasn't His responsibility. He exercised His authority with humility, and that is the genius of Jesus.

How many arguments would that end?

How many conflicts would that resolve?

How many relationships would that reconcile?

Pilate did the exact opposite. He washed his hands as a way of saying, "It's not my responsibility." Of course, this denial of responsibility is as old as Cain's disclaimer: "Am I my brother's keeper?"[10]

"Pilate was merciful," said C. S. Lewis, "till it became risky."[11] He knew Jesus was innocent, but Pilate was a people pleaser! "Wanting to satisfy the crowd, Pilate released Barabbas to them."[12]

As a recovering people pleaser, can I share a few lessons learned?

An insult from a fool may actually be a compliment, and a compliment from a fool may be an insult. Consider the source! Pilate was afraid of the wrong people, the religious leaders. He gave in to a trending hashtag: "Crucify him!"[13]

My advice? *Thou shalt offend Pharisees!* Jesus did it with great regularity and intentionality. He could have healed on any other day of the week, but He chose the Sabbath. Why? Why not kill two birds with one stone! Heal the man born blind and confront the self-righteousness of the Pharisees while you're at it.[14]

There is a proverb that I found troubling for many years because it seemed to be contradictory, but truth is found in the tension of opposites. "Don't answer the foolish arguments of fools," says Proverbs 26:4 (NLT). The very next verse says, "Be sure to answer the foolish arguments of fools." Well, which is it? Answer or don't answer? I hate to break it to you, but if you're dealing with a fool, it's a no-win situation! You're damned if you do, damned if you don't. You can please some of the people all the time or all the people some of the time, but you can't please all the people all the time!

I don't care if your name is Moses and you come down Mount Sinai with stone tablets inscribed by the finger of God— you will still encounter resistance. It's the diffusion of innovation bell curve. On one end of the bell curve, 16 percent of people will be early adopters. We love early adopters because they jump on the bandwagon, no questions asked. On the other end of the bell curve are the 16 percent of people who are called laggards.[15] They tend to resist change, and that's frustrating for leaders. But I've come to appreciate the resisters because they help refine vision!

If you're dealing with a laggard, you'll have to say please a few more times! Their natural inclination is no, and you can't hold that against them. That's the way they're wired. That doesn't excuse cynicism or skepticism, which are nice words for a lack of faith. Delayed obedience is disobedience, so I'm not giving a free pass to the cynics out there. But our *please* has to accommodate the personality of those we're asking!

"Don't let an arrow of criticism pierce your heart," Erwin McManus said at a conference years ago, "unless it first passes through the filter of Scripture." If it passes through that filter, you need to repent. No one is above reproach! If it doesn't pass through the filter, don't let a seed of bitterness take root in your spirit. Why are we so quick to accept criticism from people we wouldn't accept advice from?

My advice? Live for the applause of nail-scarred hands! If you live on compliments, you'll die by criticism. Nine times out of ten, criticism is the lazy way out. Criticize by creating! Write a better book. Produce a better film. Draft better legislation. Start a better business. How? With the help of the Holy Spirit.

Who are you afraid of offending? If you're afraid of offending people, you'll offend God. If you're afraid of offending God, you'll offend people. You can't have it both ways!

Are you washing your hands? Or washing feet?

> Jesus knew that the Father had put all things under his power, and that he had come from God and was returning to God; so he got up from the meal, took off his outer clothing, and wrapped a towel around his waist.[16]

When you recognize that everything you have—time, talent, and treasure—is a gift from God, you don't have to put on airs. You're freed up to wash other people's feet. Why? You recognize that it's all from God and it's all for God. *Please* doesn't assert its authority. It relinquishes its rights. It takes responsibility instead of shifting blame. *Please* is putting a towel around our waist and washing feet.

Our natural instinct is to get the upper hand, but that turns into an endless game of one-upmanship. Speaking of the upper hand, how you shake hands may say more about you than you realize. First of all, a firm handshake conveys confidence and respect. A weak handshake conveys anxiety and timidity. My advice? Go in strong, and make eye contact while you're at it. But there is one subtlety that is even more significant. If you shake hands with your palm angled downward, it communicates dominance. If you shake hands with your palm angled upward, it communicates submission. It may not seem like a big deal, but like first-person pronouns, it speaks volumes.

Please is giving someone else the upper hand. It's a posture of humility. It's setting aside your preferences. It's giving someone else the first right of refusal. *Please* is shaking hands, palm up. The greatest of all, said Jesus, is the servant of all.[17] Maybe, just maybe, the person with the most power should say please the most.

Remember Saul? His insecurity caused him to build monuments to himself. Washing feet is the exact opposite! Jesus had zero insecurity! He knew that His authority came from God, and that allowed Him to operate with a spirit of humility.

Jesus told His disciples that instead of calling shotgun and taking the seat of honor, they should take the lowest seat. In other words, shake hands with your palm angled upward. Even if it's within your power to get your way, say please. Take nothing for granted. Why? You live on borrowed time. You breathe borrowed breath. Even your talent is on loan from God. Potential is God's gift to you. What you do with it is your gift back to God.

We have a saying at NCC: *Fill the gaps with positive assumptions.* Give people the benefit of the doubt. Does it always work out? Absolutely not. People will disappoint you. But generally speaking, people live up or live down to our expectations. No one was better at spotting potential than Jesus! Why? He's the one who gave people that potential in the first place.

How are you treating people?

Are you giving them something to live up to?

Or are you giving them something to live down to?

We have a thirteen-pound cockapoo named Nella who is as cute as they come. She doesn't just wag her tail; she wags her entire body! If I'm gone for five minutes, she wags her body like she hasn't seen me in weeks. Guess what? That dog has me wrapped around her paw. Why? She greets me with such genuine love, it's impossible not to love her! You don't have to roll over or wag your body when you meet people, but we could learn a thing or two from man's best friend.

"If anyone, then, knows the good they ought to do and doesn't do it, it is sin for them."[18] More specifically, it's a sin of omission. And there are no loopholes! Quit washing your hands and pretending it's someone else's problem. Start washing feet, and see whether doors don't open sesame! *Please* is *not* people pleasing. It takes a ton of courage to grab a towel and wash feet, but when you do, your *please* packs a punch!

Are you washing your hands of responsibility?

Or are you taking responsibility and washing feet?

5
Words Matter

Caring for language is a moral issue.
—MARILYN MCENTYRE,
Caring for Words in a Culture of Lies

Paul Tournier, the Swiss physician and counselor, told of a patient he treated who felt a chronic sense of unworthiness, an acute sense of emptiness. During counseling, the woman shared an incident from her childhood when she overheard her mother say to her father, "We could have done without that one!"[1] Those words were an open wound decades later. They were more than careless words; they were a curse.

All of us have shame scripts—*I am unwanted, unworthy, unlovable.* A blessing can flip the script the other way. Remember, our words create worlds. One prophetic word can rewrite an entire narrative! Either way, our words have a ripple effect.

In his Hall of Fame speech, Brett Favre told a story he had never shared publicly. In high school, Favre's father was also his football coach. After a game when he didn't play particularly well, he sat outside his dad's office and overheard him talking to the other coaches: "I can assure you one thing about my son:

He will play better. He will redeem himself. I know my son. He has it in him."

I think it's fair to say that Brett Favre played better, all the way to the Pro Football Hall of Fame. "I never forgot that statement," he said. "I spent the rest of my career trying to redeem myself."[2] All of us need someone who believes in us more than we believe in ourselves. For Brett Favre, it was a father who didn't give up on him.

For better or for worse, our words are self-fulfilling prophecies. Are you giving people something to live up to or something to live down to? Are your words life-giving? Or do your words suck the life out of others? Are your words encouraging or discouraging?

I don't know what you do for a living, but you, my friend, are a prophet. Your words matter. Your words carry weight. You have the power to speak life or speak death. Could I be so bold as to add a hyphen to your occupation? I don't care what you do; you are a doctor-prophet, a teacher-prophet, a barista-prophet, an Uber-driver-prophet. The same is true of parents. Prayer turns ordinary parents into prophets who shape the destinies of their children. Remember the pastor who spoke prophetically over my life? That was the first and last time I ever met him, but he changed the trajectory of my life with ten words: "God is going to use you in a great way."

In Hebrew, *lashon hara* denotes derogatory speech that damages another person. It's expressly forbidden to speak or listen to such language. The first instance of lashon hara happened when the serpent slandered the goodness of God in the Garden of Eden. The spies who brought back a negative report of the Promised Land were guilty of lashon hara. They spoke words against God, and the entire nation lost heart. Their negativity cost them an entire generation!

Can I make a confession? I'm better at complaining than confronting! It's so much easier, isn't it? It's okay to verbalize what you're feeling, but there is a fine line between processing and gossiping. If you cross the line, it's lashon hara.

When the Israelites were wandering in the wilderness, Aaron and Miriam got frustrated with Moses. "Miriam and Aaron began to talk against Moses."[3] God heard them, and Miriam ended up with leprosy. Was it psychosomatic? I'm not sure. But if our words create worlds, then our external realities are affected by our internal attitudes. The Jewish people weren't allowed to speak lashon hara. They weren't allowed to listen to lashon hara either. Why? Because words have incredible power.

There is a Jewish story about a woman who visited a rabbi and confessed to spreading falsehoods about another person. The rabbi gave her two tasks. The first task was to take feathers from a pillow and put one at the doorstep of every home in the village. After doing this, she returned to the rabbi and said, "What's the second task?" The rabbi said, "Go and gather up all the feathers from each of the houses." "But, Rabbi, that's impossible," the woman objected. "The wind has spread them far and wide." "Indeed it has," said the rabbi. "To gather those feathers is as impossible as taking back the harsh words you have spoken. You would do well to remember that before you speak in the future."

This goes without saying, but there are some things you shouldn't say! When God called Jeremiah to be His prophet, Jeremiah objected: "I do not know how to speak; I am too young."[4] If you're looking for an excuse, you'll always find one!

You'll never be enough of *this*. You'll always be too much of *that*. God doesn't call the qualified; He qualifies the called.

God gave Jeremiah a gag order: "Do not say, 'I am too young.'"[5] Why? Because, in so doing, Jeremiah was reinforcing a wrong narrative! He was speaking words that were contrary to God's plans and purposes, which is lashon hara. "You must go to everyone I send you to and say whatever I command you."[6]

There is a phrase—*my word is my bond*—that traces back to Shakespearean times. But the idea goes further back than that. "Let your 'Yes' be 'Yes,'" Jesus said, "and your 'No,' 'No.'"[7] In other words, say what you mean and mean what you say. We waste words, don't we? Or worse, we don't really mean what we say! But there is a high value, a high standard, placed on words: "By your words you will be acquitted, and by your words you will be condemned."[8]

Francis Schaeffer once noted that if we were all forced to wear a voice recorder that captured all our conversations and if those conversations were made public for the whole world to hear, all of us would go into hiding for the rest of our lives![9]

All of us have said things we regret. Beating yourself up over it won't make it better! But I would recommend an honest evaluation of your words. What would a transcript of your conversations say about you? Are there any words that need to be deleted from your vocabulary? Is there a body posture you need to change? How about tone? One small change could alter the trajectory of your life!

Remember my confession in the introduction? I was using negative words with a high degree of frequency, and they were becoming self-fulfilling prophecies. I was committing lashon hara against myself. If you struggle with negative self-talk, give yourself a gag order!

Let no foul or polluting language, nor evil word nor unwhole-some or worthless talk [ever] come out of your mouth, but only such [speech] as is good and beneficial to the spiritual progress of others, as is fitting to the need and the occasion, that it may be a blessing and give grace (God's favor) to those who hear it.[10]

It's time to take inventory.
Are your words reconciling or dividing?
Are your words encouraging or discouraging?
Are your words helpful or hurtful?
Are your words blessing or cursing?

Some of the saddest words in the Bible belong to Esau, right after Jacob stole his blessing. "Do you have only one blessing, my father?"[11] Esau was a man's man. His name literally means "hairy." He probably shaved twice a day! Esau wasn't touchy feely, but Scripture says he wept out loud. "Bless me, even me also, O my father."[12]

Blessing is the deepest longing of the human heart. Why? It's our oldest collective memory! The first thing God did after creating humankind in His image was to bless them: "Then God blessed them."[13] Original blessing precedes original sin, and that sequence is not insignificant. It sets the tone. It sets the table. God's default setting is blessing! Blessing is His most ancient instinct. It's who God is. It's what God does.

"What comes into our minds when we think about God," said A. W. Tozer, "is the most important thing about us."[14] What comes to mind? What is God's posture toward you? What expression is God wearing on His face? What is His tone of voice when He speaks?

In the beginning, God created us in His image. Unfortunately, we've been creating God in our image ever since! It's called anthropomorphism. When we project our predisposi- tions and prejudices, our inclinations and imperfections, onto God, we end up with a god who looks a lot like us! It's a false image, an idol.

If God has a frown on His face, I think you're projecting your frustration. If God has smile lines around His eyes, if God is reaching toward you with arms wide open, I think you're get- ting much closer to the truth! If we had better hearing, we'd hear the heavenly Father singing over us with joy.[15] If we had better hearing, we'd hear Him say, "This is my beloved Son, in whom I am well pleased."[16] That certainly goes for His daugh- ters too!

Please is a posture of humility, first and foremost. It doesn't take anything for granted. Not a whiff of entitlement. It places high value on others. It creates a culture of honor, a culture of respect. Instead of tit for tat, *please* passes the peace.

> When you enter the home, give it your blessing. If it turns
> out to be a worthy home, let your blessing stand; if it is not,
> take back the blessing.[17]

Those are the instructions Jesus gave His disciples when He sent them out on their inaugural mission, and once again, the sequence is significant. Most of us operate in the opposite way. Before offering someone our blessing, we do a quick moral cal- culation. We try to figure out whether that person is worthy of the blessing *before* we give it. Right? Jesus took the opposite tack. He led with blessing, and He calls us to follow suit.

In computer science, a default setting is one that is automatically assigned to a software program. As Jesus followers, the Sermon on the Mount is our operating system. And blessing is our default setting! Remember the six counterintuitive instructions? They are worth repeating! We are called to love our enemies, pray for those who persecute us, and bless those who curse us. We turn the other cheek, go the extra mile, and give the shirts off our backs.

What does any of that have to do with *please*? More than meets the eye! We don't lead with our opinions or agenda. We don't even lead with *me*. *Please* is putting other people first. Our objective is adding value to others, and it starts with blessing!

Please is checking your ego at the door.

Please is filling the gaps with positive assumptions.

Please is catching people doing things right.

Please is bragging about people behind their backs.

Please is loving everybody always.[18]

The Hebrew word for "bless" is *barak,* and it means "to speak words of excellence about." Remember the woman who broke open her alabaster jar of perfume and anointed Jesus? The religious leaders berated both her and Jesus. "If this man were a prophet, he would know who is touching him and what kind of woman she is—that she is a sinner."[19] The religious leaders were always writing people off. Why? They focused on what was wrong. All they saw were presenting problems! A true prophet sees potential where others see problems, and no one was better at seeing potential than Jesus. Jesus counteracted their criticism with these life-giving, life-altering words: "Wherever the gospel is preached throughout the world, what she has done will also be told, in memory of her."[20] Can you imagine the way those words buoyed her spirit the rest of her life? Those are the kinds of words you have inscribed on your tombstone! Jesus blessed her with prophetic words, and they were fulfilled one more time with your reading of them!

Can I ask a question? What is the loudest voice in your life? Is it your inner critic? The cynical voice of culture? The condemning voice of the Enemy? Or is it the still, small voice of the Holy Spirit?

You will become who you listen to! According to Laurie Beth Jones, at least 40 percent of our lives are based on personal prophecies.[21] We are profoundly shaped, for better or for worse, by what's said about us. Why not give God the last word? While you're at it, why not give God the first word?

Do you know why I do a daily Bible reading plan? I need to be primed by God's promises. I need to be grounded in God's good, pleasing, and perfect will. That's one way we overwrite the negative narratives propagated by social media and the news media. Scripture is our script-cure, and that's more than a play on words. That's the power of God's Word.

I have a friend who started having panic attacks that came out of nowhere. He had never experienced anything like that, so he wasn't sure what to do. That's when he picked up a book by Randy Frazee, *His Mighty Strength*. In that book, Frazee told a story about a very similar struggle he had faced decades before. He was paralyzed by an irrational anxiety that something bad was going to happen to his kids. The cure was a cassette tape his counselor gave him. Frazee started listening to the Bible for thirty minutes twice a day, and it helped him overcome his anxiety. "Psychotherapists call it neurolinguistic programming," said his counselor, "but I call it biblical meditation."[22] The psalmist said it this way: "Thy word have I hid in mine heart, that I might not sin against thee."[23]

If your psychology needs some adjusting, Psalms is a pretty good prescription. A regular diet of God's Word will rewrite the negative narratives that sabotage your success. After reading Frazee's book, my friend did something similar. He asked his mom and dad, who are in their seventies, to record themselves reading Scripture. He now listens to those recordings as he tries to fall asleep. My friend is in his forties, but you're never too old for bedtime Bible stories!

Everything God created is good, and nothing is to be rejected if it is received with thanksgiving, because it is consecrated by the word of God and prayer.[24]

We are consecrated by two things: the Word of God and prayer. Prayer has a way of purifying our motives and sanctifying our expectations. Pray it before you say it. Yes, that includes *please*! Few things are more powerful than a prayerful *please*.

The bigger the ask, the more you need to pray! Prayer will produce bold humility or humble boldness—take your pick! Your *please* will pack a punch because it's been submitted to God.

In the same sense, the Word of God has a consecrating effect on us. Why? It's living and active! You don't just read the Bible; the Bible reads you. It penetrates the soul. It reveals the attitudes of the heart.[25]

All Scripture is God-breathed and is useful for teaching, rebuking, correcting and training in righteousness.[26]

The Holy Spirit is on both sides of the question. He inspired the original writers, but He also quickens us as readers. It's almost like we're inhaling what the Holy Spirit exhaled thousands of years ago!

I have read thousands of books, but the Bible is in a category by itself. God is watching over His Word to perform it.[27] His Word doesn't return void.[28] I have a bookmark in my Bible that says, "Whatever keeps me from my Bible is my enemy, however harmless it may appear."

There are some things you shouldn't say, and there are other things you should. "Faith cometh by hearing, and hearing by the word of God."[29] There is power in the spoken word, especially a declaration of faith.

If you confess with your mouth Jesus as Lord, and believe in your heart that God raised Him from the dead, you will be saved.[30]

Have you made a confession of sin?
Have you made a declaration of faith?
Why not do it right here, right now?

Part 2

THE SCIENCE OF *SORRY*

In 2002, Daniel Kahneman was awarded a Nobel Prize for his groundbreaking work in the field of behavioral economics. In his acceptance letter to the Nobel Committee, he detailed a defining moment that inspired his work. In 1942, the Kahneman family was living in German-occupied France. Being Jews, they were required to wear the yellow Star of David on their clothing. For eight-year-old Danny, the stigma of that star produced overwhelming shame. He would walk to school a half hour early so the other students wouldn't see it.

One night Danny was out past curfew when he encountered a German SS soldier. He tried to hurry by because he was scared of what the soldier might do, but the soldier stopped him anyway. Then that soldier did something that Danny had no category for, something that would change the trajectory of his life. The soldier opened his wallet, showed Danny a picture of his son, and gave him some money.

"There is always one moment in childhood," said the English author Graham Greene, "when the door opens and lets the future in."[1] This was that moment for Daniel Kahneman. He said, "I went home more certain than ever that my mother was right: people were endlessly complicated and interesting."[2]

How do you see people?

If you see people as uninteresting, you will mistreat them. You will demean and devalue. You will use and abuse. You will see them as stepping stones, a means to an end. And you will find it hard to forgive and seek forgiveness.

If you see people as "endlessly complicated and interest-ing," you will honor them as invaluable and irreplaceable. Of course, you have to see past first impressions. You have to cul-tivate a holy curiosity that asks lots of questions.

Did you know that the average child asks 125 questions per day? The average adult asks six! Somewhere between child-hood and adulthood, we lose 119 questions per day.[3] How do we recapture the holy curiosity of childhood? By taking a learn-ing posture in every interaction. "Every man I meet is my supe-rior in some way," said Ralph Waldo Emerson, "and in that, I learn from him."[4] You've never met anyone you can't learn from. But if you want to glean wisdom, you'll have to do more listening than talking, which is easier said than done.

The average person spends about 95 percent of their time thinking about themselves.[5] That leaves only 5 percent of our time and attention to focus on others! Could we at least dou-ble that? What if we devoted 10 percent of our time to think-ing about, caring about, learning about others? Time is as hard to tithe as money, but if we doubled down on focusing on others, I think we'd be twice as happy! After all, happiness is the opposite of self-absorption.

When we focus on ourselves, our problems are magnified. One of the best ways to solve our problems is to serve others! That may sound like correlation without causation, but serv-ing others puts our problems in perspective. "No man can sin-cerely try to help another without helping himself," said Emerson.[6]

For nearly two decades, our family has packed brown-bag lunches for our friends experiencing homelessness. It's a small token of love, but Jesus said that giving someone a cup of water in His name matters.[7] We do it to help our friends, but we feel like the primary beneficiaries. It's a visceral reminder that if you've got a roof over your head and food on your table, you're blessed.

There is a phenomenon called the illusion of asymmetrical insight. It's a cognitive bias whereby we perceive our knowledge of others to be greater than their knowledge of themselves. We thin-slice people. We judge the book by its cover. I have a friend named Scooby who spent many years living on the streets of D.C. "We take one thing," says Scooby, "and make it the whole thing." It's true, isn't it? It's a lot easier to hold opinions about people than it is to have empathy for them!

Here's the bottom line: *Everyone is fighting a battle you know nothing about.* When someone says something or does something that hurts me, I try to remember that. Hurt people hurt people. That doesn't excuse bad behavior, but it does put it in perspective. And it helps me respond the same way Jesus did: "Father, forgive them, for they know not what they do."[8]

In 2021, an artist named Suzanne Firstenberg and her team were commissioned to create an art installation on the National Mall. They planted 695,000 flags near the Washington Monument to commemorate those who had died from Covid-19. A photographer named Stephen Wilkes took a picture of that installation, but it's no ordinary photo. It's actually 4,882 snapshots that Wilkes blended together digitally, part of his *Day to Night* series. If you haven't seen it, it's worth googling.

Stephen Wilkes had to find the right vantage point from which to photograph. It had to be high enough to get a bird's-eye view. It had to be low enough to capture body language and emotion. Wilkes set up a forty-five-foot perch that could capture the epic scale of the twenty-acre installation. He wanted the National Museum of African American History and Culture to be a focal point, so you can see the sun rising over it. Along with capturing the big picture, he also captured, in his words, "little moments, little vignettes." The result is a composite photograph that gives a panoramic view.[9]

When you meet someone, it's like seeing a single snapshot. If you aren't careful, you'll judge the book by its cover. *Sorry* is more akin to a composite photograph. It captures the nuance of little details, but it also captures context via the big picture.

My point? Everyone you meet is a composite. They are a complex combination of defense mechanisms and adaptive strategies. The most common strategy? It's a toss-up between fight and flight. We either attack or retreat. There is a better way, the Jesus way, and it starts with *sorry*. Every apology begins with empathy. It's a heart that breaks for the things that break the heart of God.

"Three-fourths of the people you will ever meet are hungering and thirsting for sympathy," said Dale Carnegie. "Give it to them, and they will love you."[10] People want to feel seen, heard, and understood.

A fascinating study suggests that those who read fiction are less prejudiced and more empathetic.[11] Why? The working theory is that fiction readers are better at putting themselves in other people's shoes. That's what you do when you read a novel, right? Fiction increases our empathy for others and expands our imaginations. Of course, the same thing happens when you listen to someone share their story!

One day while fighting in the Spanish Civil War, George Orwell had an unexpected encounter with an enemy soldier. The famed English author had gone to fight fascism, but when this enemy soldier ran across the battlefield holding his pants up in the air, Orwell refused to shoot. Why? "I did not shoot partly because of that detail about the trousers," Orwell later reflected. "I had come here to shoot at 'Fascists'; but a man who is holding up his trousers isn't a 'Fascist,' he is visibly a fellow creature, similar to yourself, and you don't feel like shooting at him."[12]

In his book *Humanity*, Jonathan Glover referred to moments like these as breakthroughs of sympathy.[13] Even in the context of war, there are acts of compassion that transcend the conflict. Most of those breakthroughs are triggered by eye-to-eye contact, which defuses hand-to-hand combat by restoring heart-to-heart connection. That's what a simple *sorry* can accomplish, in words or tears. It can breach the dam of unforgiveness.

Again, hurt people hurt people. Instead of dealing with their hurt, they repress it. Repression is like trying to keep a fully inflated beach ball beneath the surface of the water. Those repressed feelings will surface sooner or later, usually at the most inopportune time. We have to cast our cares on God. Confession lets the air out of those emotions—it's letting go and letting God forgive us. Then we return the favor by forgiving others.

The bottom line? Forgiven people forgive people, seventy times seven.[14] That's how we return the favor of forgiveness. We show God's amazing grace to others. And forgiving others sets us free. "When we forgive," said Lewis Smedes, "we set a prisoner free and then discover that the prisoner we set free was us."[15]

Without empathy, our apologies are empty. Saying sorry

without feeling sorry sends mixed signals. Are you or aren't you sorry? You have to own the apology!

In one season of life and ministry, I was so pressed by my responsibilities as a pastor that a few priorities got out of whack. I'm embarrassed to admit this, but I was too busy to be bothered by family problems. That caused a deep wound for Lora. During a day of prayer many years later, the Holy Spirit surfaced that moment, that memory. With tears in her eyes, Lora said, "I forgive you." Lora needed to say it, and I needed to hear it. It didn't change the mistakes I'd made, but it brought tremendous healing. And, I might add, a renewed resolve to be fully present.

6

Try Tears

When you move past self,
life is simpler and less stressful.
—TOM RATH, *It's Not About You*

In 1543, the Polish polymath Nicolaus Copernicus published a book that identified the sun as the center of our solar system. Until that point, it was widely assumed that everything in the universe revolved around the earth. Copernicus's heliocentric cosmology turned the world upside down and inside out. All of us need what I would call a Copernican revolution. Why? We're way too self-centered.

When we're babies, our parents feed us, burp us, and change our diapers. The world revolves around us, right? And that's okay at first. If it still revolves around you at seventeen, thirty-seven, or seventy-seven, you need a Copernican revolution. News flash: It's not about you. The sooner we discover that fact, the happier, healthier, and holier we will be.

Marriage is one of the most effective ways of combating our built-in selfishness. Its purpose is not just happiness; it's holiness. Marriage is an unconditional commitment to an imperfect person. You vow to love each other for better or for worse, for richer or for poorer, in sickness and in health. You switch pronouns from *me* to *we*.

If marriage doesn't dismantle our selfishness, God gives some of us kids! Fun fact? The word *diaper* spelled backward is *repaid*. When you have children, you start appreciating your parents, don't you? They made more sacrifices, like feeding you in the middle of the night, than you were aware of.

What does any of that have to do with *sorry*?

Marriage is a master class in the art of apologizing! You might as well get good at it because you'll be doing it the rest of your marriage! The same goes for parenting. You'll have endless opportunities to say sorry to your children, and that may be a blessing in disguise. We beat ourselves up over the mistakes we make, but our biggest mistakes double as our greatest opportunities. How will our kids learn to apologize if we don't model it for them?

If you're self-absorbed, you'll see other people as obstacles to get around or inconveniences to endure. You'll use them as a means to an end. Historically speaking, we have a bad habit of objectifying people and personifying objects.

Remember the study from chapter 1? When testosterone levels go up, our use of social pronouns—*we, us, they, them*—goes down. Why? We become more task-oriented and less relationship-oriented. Instead of a win-win mindset, we turn everything into a competition. That is a zero-sum game, but no one really wins in the end.

Can I let you in on a little secret? Selfish people don't say sorry. Why? They haven't learned to put themselves in other people's shoes. Instead of washing feet like Jesus, they wash their hands like Pilate. They deny responsibility. They shift the blame. They play the victim and they play God.

Along with self-centeredness, we suffer from self-consciousness. In my opinion, an unhealthy self-consciousness is a by-product of the curse. Before the Fall, Adam and Eve were naked and knew no shame. After original sin, shame entered the equation. They became so tangled up in self-consciousness that they hid from God and each other. We've been playing hide-and-seek ever since! Part of the sanctification process is overcoming our self-consciousness. How? By becoming more God-conscious and others-conscious.

Let me double back to Daniel Kahneman. Remember the lesson his mother taught him? People are endlessly complicated and interesting! What you see is *not* what you get. So quit judging the book by its cover! It bears repeating: *Everyone is fighting a battle you know nothing about.* We draw conclusions too quickly, especially negative conclusions. If someone ticks us off, we write them off. I'm not excusing bad behavior, but is it possible they're having an off day?

I like to think of people as a 28,124-piece jigsaw puzzle. That's the average lifespan of a human in days.[1] Each of us is a unique combination of experiences and influences. In the words of Morrie Schwartz, "I am every age, up to my own."[2]

What is your earliest memory?

Who left their fingerprints on your soul?

Was there a moment in childhood when the door opened and let the future in?

What is your greatest regret?

Your greatest accomplishment?

What are the defining moments of your life?

The defining decisions?

Your answers to those questions are unlike anyone else's, and that's the tip of the iceberg. It's your unique history that differentiates you from everyone else on the planet. If we took the time to listen to other people's backstories, we would be filled with far more compassion for each other. We might even see some untapped potential.

Each of us is a complex combination of adaptive strategies. Most of us tend toward one of two strategies: aggression or regression. We either attack or retreat, but there is a better way, the Jesus way. And it starts with *sorry*. *Sorry* may sound like waving a white flag, but it's quite the opposite. It's getting out of your trench and walking into the line of fire. Few things take more courage than saying sorry!

Sorry is a *we* word. It mends broken fences. It builds bridges across relational divides. And it levels the playing field. But it has to pass a twofold litmus test: It has to be specific, and it has to be sincere.

Have you ever tried to end an argument by saying sorry even though you have no idea what you're sorry for? Me too! Occasionally, Lora will call my bluff by asking me what I'm sorry for. Sometimes I have no clue! I just want the argument to end. Let's be real, though: That's an empty apology. Why? If you don't know what you're sorry for, you'll do it all over again. It doesn't pass the specificity test.

Lord, forgive me for everything I did wrong.

Can God do that? Of course He can, but that's a half-hearted apology. Don't be surprised if you don't feel forgiven! A nebulous confession can result in a nebulous sense of forgiveness.

Many years ago, I was invited to a gathering of leaders in Wittenberg, Germany. That's where a priest named Martin Luther nailed his Ninety-Five Theses to the doors of the Castle Church. On the way there, I read a biography about Luther that noted that he would spend up to six hours at a time in confession. I couldn't remember spending more than six minutes!

> Every sin in order to be absolved was to be confessed. Therefore the soul must be searched and the memory ransacked and the motives probed.[3]

I'm not suggesting we fixate on every mistake we make, but we could probably afford to do a little more searching and ransacking and probing! Just as a nebulous confession will result in a nebulous sense of forgiveness, a nuanced confession will result in a nuanced sense of forgiveness. If you don't get to the root issue, you'll be confessing the same symptoms over and over again.

The writer of Lamentations said that God's mercies are "new every morning."[4] The Hebrew word for "new" is *hadas*. It doesn't just mean "new" as in "again and again," which would be amazing in and of itself. It means "new" as in "different." It means "never experienced before." Today's mercy is different from yesterday's mercy! Like snowflakes, God's mercy never crystallizes the same way twice. Every act of mercy is unique.

Imagine an old European city with narrow cobbled streets and storefronts as old as the city itself. One of those weathered storefronts has a sign hanging over the door: The Mercy Shop. There's no lock on the door because it's never closed. There's no cash register because mercy is free. When you ask for mercy, the Owner of the shop takes your measurements, then disappears into the back. Good news—He's got your size! Mercy is never out of stock, never out of style! As you walk out the door, the Owner of the Mercy Shop smiles. "Thanks for coming!" With a wink, He says, "I'll see you tomorrow!"

Mercy is tailored to your sin, your circumstances. It fits like a glove! But you have to be willing to share your measurements with the Tailor. Grace is also custom fit, but it's distinct from mercy. Mercy is not getting what you deserve. Grace is getting what you don't deserve.

Here's another important distinction.

We confess our sin to God for *forgiveness*.

We confess our sin to each other for *healing*.

Confess your sins to each other and pray for each other so that you may be healed.[5]

As a pastor, I've heard lots of confessions. Some of them have caught me by surprise. But I can honestly say that my respect level for the person making the confession always goes up. Why? I'm not shocked by sin. I'm shocked by those who actually have the courage to confess it to someone else. And once it's out in the open, the Enemy can't blackmail you anymore. That is when and where and how breakthrough happens!

Along with the specificity test, every confession has to pass the sincerity test. If you do the right thing for the wrong reasons, it doesn't count in the kingdom of God. Ultimately, God judges the motives of our hearts.

In psychology, there is something called *exposure therapy*. Instead of avoiding the things we're afraid of, we expose ourselves to them in safe environments, in safe ways. We face our fears with the goal of building up a measure of immunity to them. I'm taking a little bit of liberty, but in my book, vulnerability is a form of exposure therapy. It doesn't hide its imperfections. It plays a risk chip by authentically sharing hurts, habits, and hang-ups. Once you reveal it, God can begin to heal it. And in my experience, people respond to vulnerability more positively than to authority!

An apology will be effective only if you genuinely mean it. You have to check your motives. Are you trying to get something off your chest? Does your confession have more to do with relieving your guilt than restoring the relationship? Or do you have the other person's best interests at heart? Speaking from experience, an insincere apology compounds the fracture. You have to say what you mean and mean what you say. That said, a sincere *sorry* can move mountains of pain, shame, and regret. It can roll away forty years of reproach.[6] It can restore what the locusts have stolen.[7] It can even save a nation.

The unsung hero in the book of Exodus is Pharaoh's daughter. She went to the Nile to bathe, but she ended up fostering a Hebrew baby. How? She found the basket that Moses had been placed in by his birth mother.

She opened it and saw the baby. He was crying, and she felt sorry for him.[8]

Did you catch that? She felt sorry.

It was her father who ordered the killing of Hebrew babies, so she was risking her life by saving Moses. Saving that baby was her way of apologizing for her family's genocide. Here's what I know for sure: A single *sorry* saved a life, saved a nation. And take note—it started with tears!

What are the most moving moments in the metanarrative of

Scripture? What are the tipping points, the turning points? Some would say the miracles, and it's hard to argue with that. Others would point to the teachings of Jesus in the Gospels. But I believe the key incidents usually involve tears!

What did Joseph do when he was reunited with his brothers? He wept.[9] How about Esau when he was betrayed by Jacob? He wept.[10] What did Peter do after denying Jesus? He wept bitterly.[11] What did Jesus do when He came to the tomb of Lazarus?

It's the shortest verse in the Bible, but it speaks volumes: "Jesus wept."[12]

Those tears represent different things, ranging from repentance to regret. In the case of Jesus, it's holy empathy.

Tears are liquid empathy.

Tears are liquid prayers.

In the early 1900s, Kate and Mary Jackson tried to establish a Salvation Army in the city of Leeds, but nothing seemed to work. Disappointed and discouraged by their lack of progress, they wrote a letter to William Booth, asking to be relocated. Booth responded with a two-word telegram: **TRY TEARS**.[13] The Jackson sisters started to travail with tears, and the Salvation Army in Leeds became one of the largest and most effective.

"The gift of tears," said Corey Russell, "is the outward sign of the inward revelation of our inability to change anything."[14] I think Russell was talking about our inability to change the past. That may sound discouraging, but it's actually liberating! You can't change what you did, period. All you can do is let it go and let God forgive you. Tears are part of that process. If you haven't cried over it, you probably haven't grieved it. Your tears are a gift from God. "They are a language all their own," said Russell. "They're the expression of a soul that's on the other side of words."[15] Like the balm of Gilead, tears have the power to heal and soothe.

Nothing says sorry like tears.

Nothing reconciles relationships like tears.

Nothing moves the heart of God like tears.

Try tears!

7

The Fifth Petition

The true saint burns grace
like a 747 burns fuel on takeoff.
—DALLAS WILLARD, *The Great Omission*

I recently had lunch with someone whose books have had a significant impact on my life. R. T. Kendall pastored Westminster Chapel in London for twenty-five years, along with authoring more than fifty books. It's hard for me to pick a favorite, but *Total Forgiveness* is a game changer. The subtitle says it all: *When Everything in You Wants to Hold a Grudge, Point a Finger, and Remember the Pain—God Wants You to Lay It All Aside.*

Easier said than done, right?

During his pastorate in London, R. T. Kendall took offense at something that had been done to him. That seed of bitterness festered as unforgiveness, and he held on to that grudge with clenched fists. He finally told a friend, aiming for a little sympathy. Much to his surprise, his friend compassionately and soberly rebuked him. "You must totally forgive them," his friend said. "I can't," Kendall objected. His friend refused to let him off the hook: "You can, and you must." It was the hardest thing

R. T. Kendall had ever had to do, but his friend was right: "Release them, and you will be set free."[1]

Is there any unforgiveness in your heart?

Has a seed of bitterness taken root?

Are you holding a grudge?

Have you taken offense?

These questions may trigger traumatic memories, so I say this with tremendous empathy: You must totally forgive. I can only imagine the things that were said, the things that were done. But unforgiveness is like drinking rat poison and thinking it will kill the rat. The only person you're hurting is yourself. You have to forgive for your sake.

Before we go any further, let me specify what forgiveness is *not*. It's not excusing bad behavior. It's not justifying injustice. It's not even pardoning what someone did. That's beyond our pay grade; only God can do that. Forgiveness is not turning a blind eye or subjecting yourself to someone else's sin. If you find yourself in an abusive or dangerous situation, you owe it to yourself and to God to get out of it. If someone commits a crime, they can experience God's grace, but that doesn't mean they won't live with the consequences of their actions. Forgiveness cancels the debt of sin, not the consequences.

The Lord's Prayer is our primer when it comes to forgiveness. In the fifth petition of the prayer, Jesus said, "Forgive us our debts, as we forgive our debtors."[2] As we all know, forgiving our debtors is easier said than done! Then Jesus doubled down with the postscript: "If you forgive other people when they sin against you, your heavenly Father will also forgive you."[3]

Our vertical forgiveness from God is connected to and contingent on our horizontal forgiveness of others. In other words, forgiveness is mandatory. That doesn't mean we become punching bags for someone else's abuse. It doesn't mean we don't establish healthy boundaries. But forgiven people forgive people. And Jesus set the standard. As He hung on the cross in excruciating pain, He somehow had the wherewithal to forgive those who nailed Him there: "Father, forgive them, for they know not what they do."[4]

When Peter asked Jesus how many times he should forgive, Jesus said, "Seventy times seven."[5] Peter's jaw must have dropped. He thought he was being gracious by offering forgiveness seven times! Jesus upped the ante, then told a story about someone who had forgiven a ten-thousand-talent debt.

One talent was worth sixty minas, and one mina was three months' wages. So one talent equaled 180 months of wages. That's fifteen years of pay! A ten-thousand-talent debt totaled 150,000 years of wages. This man owed a debt that would take 2,322 lifetimes to repay. That reminds me of the old song that says, "He paid a debt He did not owe; I owed a debt I could not pay." That calculus should give us a greater appreciation for what Christ accomplished on the cross!

Hanging on the cross, Jesus said, "It is finished."[6] It's three words in English, but it's one word in Greek: *tetelestai*. Archaeologists have found that word written across ancient receipts. It was an accounting term that means "paid in full." The Cross is the final installment on sin. Our ten-thousand-talent debt is paid in full.

God made him who had no sin to be sin for us, so that in him we might become the righteousness of God.[7]

It's almost like God says, "Here's the deal. You transfer everything you've done wrong—all your sin—to My account. I'll transfer everything Jesus did right—His righteousness—to your account. And we'll call it even." It doesn't get any better than that. That's why it's called good news.

If you are in Christ, you are justified—just as if you had never sinned. Let me paint a picture of what that looks and feels like. Remember when Peter cut off the right ear of Malchus, the servant of the high priest?[8] A group had come to arrest Jesus, so Peter pulled out a sword. To state the obvious, Peter was in a world of trouble! You don't cut off someone's ear and get by with it, especially if that someone is the high priest's servant. Worst-case scenario, Peter would get charged with attempted murder. Best-case scenario, Peter would get charged with assault and battery with a deadly weapon. Either way, he would probably end up on a cross next to Jesus.

What did Jesus do? He healed the guy who had come to arrest Him![9] Somehow He reattached his amputated ear. Good as new! But there is something bigger happening here. I love the way Dick Foth put it: "Jesus destroys the evidence against us."

Imagine Malchus filing suit against Peter. He takes the witness stand and says, "Peter cut off my ear." The judge says, "Which ear?" Malchus says, "My right one." The judge asks him to approach the bench so he can take a closer look. "It looks fine to me," the judge says. "Case dismissed." The case gets thrown out of court for lack of evidence! This isn't just a story about Peter and Malchus; it's a story about you and me. Jesus went to the cross to destroy the evidence against us!

We don't think of forgiveness as miraculous, but that's precisely what it is. Jesus turned water into wine.[10] He walked on water.[11] He healed a blind man's brain by installing a synaptic pathway between the optic nerves and visual cortex.[12] He even raised a man who was four days dead.[13] As amazing as those miracles are, His single act of forgiveness surpasses them all. In my humble opinion, this is the greatest miracle in the Gospels.

"When I truly and totally forgive," said R. T. Kendall, "I have crossed over into the supernatural—and have achieved an accomplishment equal to any miracle."[14]

Forgiveness is miraculous, but let me flip the script. It's unforgiveness that keeps us from experiencing the miraculous. Those two things may seem unrelated, so let me connect the dots. Remember when Jesus returned to Nazareth? Instead of throwing a ticker-tape parade for their favorite son, the people of Nazareth "took offense." The result? "He did not do many miracles there."[15] When you take offense, you stop playing offense. Your defense mechanisms kick in, and you start protecting your ego at all costs. It becomes a zero-sum game, and no one really wins. If you want to experience the miraculous, you have to offer forgiveness.

Michele Nelson made a distinction between three degrees of forgiveness. First-degree forgiveness is detached forgiveness—there is a reduction in negative feelings toward the offender, but no reconciliation happens. Second-degree forgiveness is limited forgiveness—there is a reduction in negative feelings toward the offender, and the relationship is partially restored, but there is a decrease in the emotional intensity of that relationship. Third-degree forgiveness is full forgiveness—there is a total cessation of negative feelings toward the offender, and the relationship is fully restored.[16]

Reconciliation is a two-way street. You can't control the other person, so you can't control the outcome. Please don't try to bear that burden! All you can control is you, and that's hard enough. I'm not sure which is more difficult: forgiving or apologizing. It's a toss-up, but here's my advice: Make the first move. Take the first step. Offer the first olive branch.

> If you are offering your gift on the altar, and there you remember that your brother or sister has something against you, leave your gift there in front of the altar. First go and be reconciled with your brother or sister, and then come and offer your gift.[17]

Let me try to put this command in context. The altar was in the temple, which was in Jerusalem. Jesus offered this advice during His Sermon on the Mount, which He delivered on the north shore of the Sea of Galilee. So what? Well, it's not like His listeners could text an apology. The altar was seventy-two miles from where He was, as the crow flies. With an average walking speed of three miles per hour, that's twenty-four hours on foot. That's on par with the Barkley Marathons. My point? There is nothing convenient about offering a sincere apology or genuinely extending forgiveness, but it's worth the trip.

Is there someone you need to forgive?

Is there something you need to confess?

What are you waiting for?

8

People of the
Second Chance

Your worst days are never so bad
that you are beyond the *reach* of God's grace.
And your best days are never so good that
you are beyond the *need* of God's grace.
Every day of our Christian experience should
be a day of relating to God on the basis
of His grace alone.
—JERRY BRIDGES, *The Discipline of Grace*

In his timeless book *The 7 Habits of Highly Effective People*, Stephen Covey told a story about riding on the subway in New York City on a Sunday morning. People were quietly minding their own business when a father entered the subway car with his children. The children started yelling at each other and throwing things. Meanwhile, the father kept his eyes closed, oblivious to the chaos his kids were causing. After exercising as much patience as possible, Covey turned to the father and said, "Sir, your children are really disturbing a lot of people. I wonder if you couldn't control them a little more?"

Suddenly aware of the situation, the father responded, "You're right. I guess I should do something about it." Then he said, "We just came from the hospital where their mother died about an hour ago. I don't know what to think, and I guess they don't know how to handle it either."[1]

In that moment, all Covey's irritation dissipated and was replaced with empathy. He experienced a paradigm shift. It's a term taken from Thomas Kuhn's groundbreaking book *The Structure of Scientific Revolutions*. Almost every breakthrough in science involves a break with tradition. It's the courage to turn the kaleidoscope. When you take time to learn a person's backstory, it reveals different patterns, and you see the person very differently. "My paradigm shifted," said Covey. "Suddenly I *saw* things differently, and because I *saw* differently, I *thought* differently, I *felt* differently, I *behaved* differently. My irritation vanished. . . . My heart was filled with the man's pain. . . . Everything changed in an instant."[2]

Like Russian nesting dolls, we all have lots of layers! If you are judgmental, people won't reveal their hidden identities or secret insecurities. You'll never get past the pretense. If you are vulnerable and reveal some of your secrets, it allows other people to open up. I think Brené Brown is right: "Staying vulnerable is a risk we have to take if we want to experience connection."[3] If you let down your guard, it gives people the freedom to reveal who they really are. That's one of the greatest gifts you can give someone. It takes radical vulnerability and holy curiosity, but it results in supernatural empathy.

In his memoir *The Sacred Journey*, Frederick Buechner wrote about the way his father's suicide affected him as a young boy. You don't *get over* that kind of traumatic experience, but you can *get through* it. "Beneath the face," said Buechner, "I am a family plot."[4] There are genetic and epigenetic factors that have consciously and subconsciously conditioned you. For better or for worse, you are an invention of your family system.

As children, we develop defense mechanisms to protect our ego. We employ adaptive strategies to get attention. As we age, those strategies may become more sophisticated. Not too many adults throw temper tantrums! But we're still driven by subliminal hopes and fears.

When you meet someone new, you know them only in real time. It's like opening a book to page 117 and starting to read. You are encountering the latest version of them, but they are endlessly complicated. They are every age up to their own! Buechner described the family burial plot beneath his face this way:

> All the people I have ever been are buried there—the bouncing boy, his mother's pride; the pimply boy and secret sensualist; the reluctant infantryman; the beholder at dawn through hospital plate-glass of his first-born child. All these selves I was I am no longer, not even the bodies they wore are my body any longer, and although when I try, I can remember scraps and pieces about them, I can no longer remember what it felt like to live inside their skin. Yet they live inside my skin to this day, they are buried in me somewhere, ghosts that certain songs, tastes, smells, sights, tricks of weather can raise, and although I am not the same as they, I am not different either because their having been then is responsible for my being now.[5]

What does that burial plot have to do with *sorry*? When you know someone's history, it helps you put them in context.

There is a simple rule in hermeneutics: *Text without context is pretext.* It's not just true of Scripture; it's true of people! Pretext is prejudice. It's coming to a conclusion before all the facts are presented.

A few years ago, I went to counseling with a therapist who specializes in family systems. I had some subliminal sadness that would surface from time to time, and I was trying to decipher it. One of the outcomes of that counseling was a greater appreciation for other people's adaptive strategies. I'm not excusing dysfunctional behavior, but it helped me understand it. Again, hurt people hurt people. All too often we protect our ego by projecting our pain.

When we meet someone whose defense mechanisms are causing collateral damage, our natural tendency is to react in kind. How do we turn the other cheek? How do we give people a second chance? It starts with holy curiosity. You need to exercise your empathy muscles by walking a mile in their shoes.

"If we could read the secret history of our enemies," said Henry Wadsworth Longfellow, "we should find in each man's life sorrow and suffering enough to disarm all hostility."[6]

I have a friend who recently hosted two high-ranking government officials from opposing parties. The high-ranking officials spent seven hours sharing their life stories with each other. Seven *hours,* not minutes! Just because you don't see eye to eye on every issue doesn't mean you can't relate heart to heart. Of course, you have to take the time to listen to another's story and ask good questions. And most of us are far too busy to do that. So we end up fighting rather than forgiving, canceling rather than caring, judging rather than empathizing. We give up on people too easily!

Instead of helping Job heal, his friends Eliphaz, Bildad, and

Zophar added insult to injury. With friends like that, who needs enemies? When someone is down, we tend to dogpile. But that's when we've got to put on our rally caps and go to bat for them. How? Pray for them!

> After Job had prayed for his friends, the LORD restored his fortunes and gave him twice as much as he had before.[7]

If someone is grieving, you don't have to solve the situation for them. In fact, you can't. What you can do is offer a sincere *sorry*. Gift them the gift of tears. Give them the gift of ears. Give them a second chance, just like God gave you.

The love of God is not reactive; it's proactive. It's not contingent upon our performance. It's an expression of who God is—God is love. There is nothing you can do to make God love you *any more* or *any less*. Why? He loves you perfectly, uniquely, and unconditionally. No one knows you better. No one loves you more.

One of my earliest memories is my elementary school principal interrupting my fourth-grade gym class and announcing over the intercom that President Ronald Reagan had been shot. The date was March 30, 1981. A would-be assassin, John Hinckley, Jr., shot the president at point-blank range outside the Washington Hilton hotel.

When we hear gunshots, the natural reaction is to protect ourselves by taking cover. Secret Service agents are trained to do the exact opposite. When Hinckley fired his .22 caliber revolver, Secret Service agent Tim McCarthy went into a spread-eagle position, making himself the largest target possible. McCarthy took a bullet for the president, probably saving his life.

Two thousand years ago, Jesus went into a spread-eagle position on the cross. He took the bullet for you and for me. "God demonstrates his own love for us in this: While we were still sinners, Christ died for us."[8]

When we're at our *worst*, God is at His *best*. God loves us when we least expect it and least deserve it. He is the God who never gives up on us. He is the God of second and third and hundredth chances. Go thou and do likewise!

9

Secret Sauce

God loves each of us as if there were only one of us.
—AUGUSTINE OF HIPPO, *Confessions*

At the turn of the twenty-first century, a unique library was established in Copenhagen, Denmark. It's called the Menneskebiblioteket, which is Danish for "the human library." Instead of checking out a book, you can have a conversation with someone who will share their story of being deaf, blind, autistic, homeless, sexually abused, or bipolar. The mission of the Human Library? To break down stereotypes and prejudices by fostering dialogue. Yes, you can ask these human books questions!

I love their motto: "Unjudge someone."

There's an idea!

Isn't that what Jesus taught in the Sermon on the Mount? "Do not judge, or you too will be judged."[1] Instead of focusing on the speck of sawdust in someone else's eye, Jesus told us to take the plank out of our own eye.[2] "You better check yourself," said Ice Cube, "before you wreck yourself."[3] How? For starters, by listening twice as much as we talk. Again, maybe that is why God gave us two ears and one mouth.

In his book, *Ask More,* Frank Sesno said, "Smart questions make smarter people."[4] The former CNN anchor detailed eleven kinds of questions. They range from confrontational questions to empathetic questions, from diagnostic questions to legacy questions. Of course, one of the most effective questions you can ask isn't even a question: "Tell me more."[5]

There are three key ingredients when it comes to question asking:

1. Ask open-ended questions that don't allow for yes or no answers.
2. Ask echo questions that get people to say something more than one time, more than one way.
3. Ask curveball questions that change the frame of reference.[6]

Along with asking questions, you've got to get vulnerable. Here's a good rule of thumb: Before you confront someone else's sin, confess your own. In the words of Tommy Boy, "Let me tell you why I suck."[7] You've got to level the playing field. One more word of advice? Compliment before you criticize! According to the Losada ratio, we need 2.9 compliments for every criticism.[8] You've got to catch people doing things right.

I subscribe to a style of leadership called appreciative inquiry. It's a strengths-based approach to change. Simply put, celebrate what you want to see more of. When you consistently compliment what people do right, it gives you ground for confronting them when they do something wrong. The letters to the seven churches in Revelation contain pointed rebukes, but they start with affirmation. That sequence is not insignificant.

When we began building out a city block as a mixed-use marketplace called the Capital Turnaround, we hired a consultant who took us through an exercise called empathy mapping. It's the first step in a human-centered design process that helps identify pain points and gain points. An empathy map asks the following questions:

What do they think?
What do they feel?
What do they see?
What do they hear?
What do they say?
What do they do?

The Incarnation is all about empathy mapping, is it not? "We do not have a high priest who is unable to empathize with our weaknesses, but we have one who has been tempted in every way, just as we are."[9] In fact, Jesus went mano a mano with the devil for forty days in the wilderness.[10]

The Word became flesh and made his dwelling among us. We have seen his glory, the glory of the one and only Son, who came from the Father, full of grace and truth.[11]

Love is grace plus truth.
Grace means "I'll forgive you no matter what."
Truth means "I'll be honest with you no matter what."
Truth minus grace is hot sauce. It's all head and no heart.

People don't care how much you know until they know how much you care.

Grace minus truth is weak sauce. It's all heart and no head. We don't want to hurt anyone's feelings, so we let them hurt themselves.

Grace plus truth is our secret sauce!

"So many of us are conditioned to avoid saying what we really think," said Kim Scott in her book *Radical Candor*. "This is partially adaptive social behavior; it helps us avoid conflict or embarrassment."[12] When we don't say what needs to be said, we fall into what Scott called ruinous empathy.[13] Love is not approving of everything someone says or does. It's not agreeing with everything someone thinks or believes. True love, tough love, cares enough to confront. It's not passive aggressive. It's not conflict avoidant. It's equal measures, full measures, of grace and truth.

The solution to ruinous empathy is radical candor, and it's two-dimensional. It's caring personally and confronting directly. The terminology may be new, but radical candor is as old as the Incarnation. And no one did it better than Jesus! He is the perfect combination of grace giving and truth telling.

John's gospel includes the story of a woman who was caught in the act of adultery. The self-righteous religious leaders wanted to stone her to death. Jesus said, "Let the one who has never sinned throw the first stone!"[14]

Brilliant, with an Irish accent. Jesus defused the hostility and came to her defense. *You can stone her, over My dead body!* He loved this woman when she least expected and, quite frankly, least deserved it. He gave her grace, but He also spoke truth. He said in no uncertain terms, "Go and sin no more."[15]

Jesus didn't excuse her behavior by sweeping it under the carpet. He called it on the carpet. But He did it in a way that was redeeming and respectful. Jesus gave her a second chance, a new lease on life. He didn't condemn or condone. He found a middle way, a third way, the Jesus way. Love doesn't compromise its convictions, but it's moved by compassion.

There is a way to disagree agreeably, but it takes humble boldness. Humility is the willingness to admit fault when you're wrong. Boldness is the willingness to risk your reputation for what's right. It takes tremendous courage to live according to your convictions, especially in a culture where it's wrong to say that something is wrong. It's choosing biblical correctness over and against political correctness.

At National Community Church, we have four principles of peacemaking that serve as guides:

1. Listen well.
2. Ask anything.
3. Disagree freely.
4. Love regardless.

Our current lack of civility in public and interpersonal discourse, along with the rise of cancel culture, is diametrically opposed to the gospel. The story of the woman caught in adultery has a subplot we easily overlook. Jesus met the qualification He established. He was without sin, but He didn't pick up a stone. Why? The answer is unadulterated grace! But notice, He also spoke the truth in love. This is the tightrope we're called to walk, and the only way we can keep our balance is by embracing both grace and truth.

In our interactions with others, there will always be disagreement. We'll disagree about who to vote for and who to root for. We'll disagree politically, aesthetically, and even theologically. How we navigate those differences reveals much about our character. Are we functioning as grace givers? Are we giving second chances? Do we try to understand other people's points of view while holding ours? Or do we write people off when we don't agree with them?

After the death of Lazarus, his sisters were grieving. Remember, words are like X-rays! They said to Jesus, "If you had been here, my brother would not have died."[16] Is it just me, or does that sound passive aggressive? It's almost like they were saying, "It's not Your fault, but it is, but it isn't, but it is." Their words were born of a deep-seated awareness that Jesus could have kept Lazarus from dying!

If your *sorry* is half-baked, don't bother.

If your *sorry* is half-hearted, stop.

If your *sorry* is passive aggressive, it'll backfire.

It seemed like Jesus was four days late, but Jesus had nothing to apologize for because it's not over until He says it's over. Don't put a period where God puts a comma! Jesus said, "Lazarus, come forth."[17]

What does raising Lazarus from the dead have to do with sorry? More than meets the eye! A simple *sorry* can have the same effect. When you give someone a second chance, it resurrects faith, hope, and love. *Sorry* is the way we remove our graveclothes.

It's time for a gut check.

Your *sorry* is only as powerful as your motives are pure.

Are you saying sorry for the other person's sake?

Or are you saying it to get it off your chest?

During the sex scandal involving President Clinton and Monica Lewinsky, Billy Graham was invited to the White House to meet with the president. Graham took some friendly fire from fellow Christians for accepting that invitation. Why? They thought he was condoning sin. Billy Graham answered his critics this way: "It's the Holy Spirit's job to convict, God's job to judge, and my job to love."

All too often, we play judge and jury. I'm certainly not suggesting that you compromise your biblical convictions. We need to speak the truth in love, without apology. That said, it's not your job to judge others. Truth be told, we tend to criticize in others what we don't like about ourselves. Or is that just me? We try to build ourselves up by putting others down. That's when and where we need to say sorry!

Would you rather be right or righteous? I'm not saying you can't be both, but if you'd rather be right, it's called self-righteousness. And it usually results in broken relationships. We sacrifice relationships on the altar of strongly held opinions. I'm not sure how else to say this: Please stop. Yes, I said please! What is it going to take to wake us up, to shake us up? The level of cynicism in our culture is out of control. The baiting and trolling have to stop. So do the blaming and shaming.

No one wins the blame game! The only way to win is to not play. The same goes for the shame game and the fame game. When you compare yourself with others, it results in pride or jealousy. You won't win either way! Comparing yourself with others is a losing battle.

Everybody is blaming everybody else for almost everything. Don't believe me? All you have to do is toggle between news stations! It's time to interrupt the pattern and try a different tactic. There is no magic bullet, but there is a magic word. *Sorry* is a good place to start. *Sorry* is the solution to a thousand problems.

What if we took less credit when things go right? What if we took more responsibility when things go wrong? What if we were a little more forgiving and a little less judgmental?

Instead of pointing fingers, it's time to look in the mirror. If you aren't part of the solution, you're part of the problem. Quit complaining about the lack of civility if you're taking potshots at others. We've got to hold ourselves to a higher standard. What is it? If we're going to be great at something, let's be great at the Great Commandment.

"Love the Lord your God with all your heart and with all your soul and with all your mind." This is the first and greatest commandment. And the second is like it: "Love your neighbor as yourself."[18]

We often think of the Greatest Commandment as two-dimensional—love God and love others. But there is a third dimension—love yourself. It sounds selfish, but it's a critical piece of the equation. It's hard to love others if you don't love yourself. How do you love yourself? You let God love you. You let God forgive you. You accept His assessment of who you are.

We make two mistakes when it comes to self-assessment. One is pride, and the other is false humility. "God opposes the proud,"[19] but false humility isn't doing anyone any favors either. It's thinking of yourself as anything less than who you are in Christ.

The hardest person to forgive is yourself. We tend to be harder on ourselves than on others. We are our own worst critics! For some reason, condemnation sinks a little deeper into the soul than commendation. That's one way our negativity bias rears its ugly head.

On that note, let me make a critical distinction. Conviction is feeling guilt over *unconfessed* sin, and it comes from the Holy Spirit. Condemnation is feeling guilt over *confessed* sin, and it comes from the Enemy! "There is now no condemnation for those who are in Christ Jesus."[20]

In his book *People of the Second Chance,* Mike Foster shared what he called the Five Condemnments. "The rules we write for ourselves are sneaky," he said. "They run quietly in the background like a virus infecting an operating system."

1. I don't deserve a second chance.
2. I am my shame. I am my secrets.
3. I will always feel and be this way.
4. I am defined by my worst moments.
5. My life, my dreams, my hopes no longer matter.[21]

If you're unable to forgive others, maybe you haven't forgiven yourself.

If not now, when?

10
Unoffendable

We should be the most refreshingly
unoffendable people on [the] planet.
—BRANT HANSEN, *Unoffendable*

When I was five years old, I put my faith in Christ
after watching a film called *The Hiding Place*. It's the life story of
Corrie ten Boom, whose family was sent to a Nazi concentration camp for hiding Jews. Ten Boom lost her father and her
sister, but she managed to survive. A few years later, she went
back to Germany to preach the good news of the gospel.

At one of those gatherings, she met a man who had been
a prison guard at the concentration camp near Ravensbrück.
When Corrie ten Boom saw his face, it triggered traumatic
memories. She remembered him as one of the cruelest guards
from the camp. The man reached out his hand and said, "A fine
message, Fraulein!" After thanking her for the message, he
made it personal: "I would like to hear it from your lips as well.
Fraulein, will you forgive me?" It was like time stood still. It was
a moment of truth. Ten Boom later recalled, "I stood there—
I whose sins had again and again been forgiven—and could not
forgive."

Forgiving that prison guard was the most difficult thing ten Boom had ever had to do. But she knew that forgiveness wasn't a function of feeling; it was an act of the will. Corrie ten Boom finally reached out her hand and took his. When she did, something miraculous happened.

> The current started in my shoulder, raced down my arm, sprang into our joined hands. And then this healing warmth seemed to flood my whole being, bringing tears to my eyes.
>
> "I forgive you, brother!" I cried. "With all my heart." . . .
>
> I had never known God's love so intensely as I did then. But even so, I realized it was not my love. I had tried, and did not have the power. It was the power of the Holy Spirit.[1]

Forty years after their exodus from Egypt, the Israelites entered the Promised Land. They camped at a place called Gilgal, on the eastern shore of the Jordan River. That is when and where God said, "Today I have rolled away the shame of your slavery in Egypt."[2] It took one day to get Israel out of Egypt, but it took forty years to get Egypt out of Israel. Forgiveness doesn't happen overnight. Sometimes it takes forty years!

When you say sorry, when you fully forgive, the reproach is rolled away. That doesn't mean you won't have setbacks or flashbacks. Salvation is a hard reset; our sin is forgiven and forgotten. We are justified, just as if we had never sinned. But forgiveness is a soft reset. It's something you need to do over and over again.

Remember my journal entry from the introduction? My head was foggy, my heart was irritated, and I felt like I was emotionally flatlining. When that check engine light came on, I knew I needed help. I started counseling, and my counselor took me through a forgiveness exercise that turned me inside out and right side up. He asked me to carve out some time and ask God a question: *Is there anyone or anything I need to forgive?* I thought it might take a few minutes. I thought wrong! The Holy Spirit began revealing unconfessed sin and unforgiven sin. I had been doing a lot more repressing than confessing. I had been doing a lot more complaining than forgiving.

I came across a comic recently that shows a man standing in a crater of his own making, having exploded on everyone around him. The caption hits close to home: "For 43 years, Hank had successfully stuffed every feeling he'd ever had, until, of course, the morning when Fred asked if he could borrow a paper clip."[3] When someone acts out of proportion to the offense, there is a good chance they aren't reacting to present-tense circumstances. They are reacting to past-tense pain. If someone is causing a lot of collateral damage—emotional, relational, spiritual—they are acting out of open wounds. That was me.

The Holy Spirit wears a lot of hats. He heals, seals, and reveals. He counsels, convicts, and comforts. One of His executive functions is surfacing subconscious motives and repressed memories.

> "What no eye has seen,
>   what no ear has heard,
> and what no human mind has conceived"—
>   the things God has prepared for those who love him—
> these are things God has revealed to us by his Spirit.
> The Spirit searches all things, even the deep things of God.[4]

The Spirit of God google searches all things. That includes the deep web of desires. That includes the dark web of motives. More than 125 trillion synapses crisscross the cerebral cortex,[5] and the Holy Spirit dwells in the forty-nanometer synaptic gap.

While I went through the forgiveness exercise my counselor prescribed, the Holy Spirit started surfacing memories. Some were recent offenses I had taken. Some were old wounds. Some were places where I needed to seek forgiveness. I had a flashback to the first time I stole something. I was at a music lesson, and I noticed that my teacher had a baseball schedule that I really wanted. I took it and never apologized. I don't think that is the unpardonable sin, but little foxes ruin the vineyard.[6] After several hours of praying and processing, I felt like I had taken off a very heavy backpack. And that's exactly what Jesus promised: "My yoke is easy and my burden is light."[7]

There are lots of reasons we don't forgive. We're afraid of getting hurt all over again. We want the other person to pay for the pain they caused. We want them to go first. We're afraid that forgiveness makes us look weak, when it's actually the opposite. Forgiveness gets rid of our built-in excuse system.

Unforgiveness is like an elastic band around your ankles. You try to make forward progress, but bitterness is holding you back. At some point, you need to cut the cord. Don't let those who hurt you define you. Quit letting them live in your head, in your heart, rent-free. Release yourself from other people's opinions. If it helps, seal the forgiveness with some kind of symbol. Release a balloon. Bury a shoebox with a description of the hurt inside it. Better yet, build a bonfire and let it burn.

Do not grieve the Holy Spirit of God, with whom you were sealed for the day of redemption. Get rid of all bitterness, rage and anger, brawling and slander, along with every form of malice. Be kind and compassionate to one another, forgiving each other, just as in Christ God forgave you.[8]

"The primary way we grieve the Spirit in our lives," said R. T. Kendall, "is by fostering bitterness in our hearts."[9] Then he flipped that script. "The absence of bitterness allows the Holy Spirit to be Himself in us. . . . When the Holy Spirit is not grieved, He is *at home* with me."[10]

If you've lost your intimacy with God, is it possible there is bitterness in your heart? If you've lost the peace that passes understanding, is it possible there is unforgiveness in your heart? If you've lost the joy of the Lord, is it possible you're holding a grudge or you've taken offense? Carve out some time, sit before the Lord, and ask the question, *Is there anyone or anything I need to forgive?*

As I see it, we have two options when it comes to the pain we inflict on others and the pain that is inflicted on us: We can repress it or we can confess it. Whatever you repress will eventually depress, and that creates the beach ball effect I've already alluded to. You can keep it submerged for a while, but it will eventually resurface. All it takes is a trigger, like Fred asking Hank for a paper clip! Unforgiveness is death by a thousand paper cuts.

In 2011, I wrote and released a book titled *The Circle Maker*. That book has sold millions of copies, and I've received thousands of testimonies from those whose prayer lives have been positively affected by it. I have to admit, I was a little shocked at some of the negative reviews I received. Trust me—I'm not looking for sympathy. Only 1 percent of reviews give it one star while 86 percent give it five stars, but those one-star reviews can weigh heavy! There were a few comments accusing me of everything from false motives to false doctrine. I even remember someone writing me and rebuking me for eating at the Cheesecake Factory. If that's wrong, I don't want to be right! In all seriousness, I had lots of people baiting me and trolling me online, but I had chosen a verse of the year that proved to be apropos.

It is to one's glory to overlook an offense.[11]

Note to self: Be careful when choosing a verse of the year— God will give you plenty of opportunities to put it into practice! I certainly didn't bat a thousand. I definitely let some things get under my skin. After all, one criticism plus one thousand compliments equals one criticism. That said, I became a lot better at being unoffendable! Why? I had made a pre-decision. No matter what others did or said, I had predetermined in my heart not to take offense.

When Stephen was stoned to death in the book of Acts, the last thing he did was kneel and pray. With his dying breath, Stephen said, "Lord, do not hold this sin against them."[12] Forgiveness isn't just a pre-decision; it's a lifelong commitment.

If you fill the gaps with negative assumptions, there is opportunity to take offense all the time! My advice? Give people the benefit of the doubt. Don't play the victim when things go bad. Don't play God when things go good.

I'm going to keep forgiving until the day I die.

I'm going to keep apologizing until the day I die.

When I was in graduate school, I was introduced to a fascinating matrix called the Johari window. *Johari* sounds fancy, but it's a combination of the first names of the two guys who came up with the matrix—Joseph Luft and Harry Ingham. It consists of four quadrants that represent four dimensions of your identity.

The first dimension is called the arena quadrant. It consists of those things *you know about yourself* and *others know about you.* It's your Facebook posts. It's your LinkedIn profile. It's who you are in public. It's what everybody sees. It's what you do forty hours a week. It's the most prominent features of your personality.

The second dimension is called the façade quadrant. It consists of those things *you know about yourself* but *others don't know about you.* This is your alter ego. This is who you are when no one is looking. It's the reality behind the curtain that hides the Wizard of Oz. This is where we feel like frauds and wrestle with imposter syndrome.

As I see it, we either develop an *alter ego,* with an *e,* or an *altar ego,* with an *a.* An alter ego is pretending to be who you're not. The problem with that is this: *If you is who you ain't, you ain't who you is!* Honestly, it's exhausting. You're never quite comfortable in your own skin. The other option? Lay your pride, your shame, your lust, your anger, your mistakes at the foot of the cross. I call it an altar ego. It's consecrating yourself—your time, talent, and treasure; your past, present, and future; your heart, soul, mind, and strength—to God.

The third dimension is called the blind-spot quadrant. It consists of those things *others know about you* but *you don't know about yourself.* This is where we need friends who care enough to confront us. This is where we need accountability partners to call us on the carpet. This is where we need a company of prophets to call out the potential within us. Of course, we need ears to hear! "Mature individuals do not resent correction," said Huston Smith. Why? "They identify more with their long-range selves that profit from correction than with the momentary self that is being advised."[13] If you have a growth mindset, you take all the correction you can get.

Finally, there is a fourth dimension called the unknown quadrant. It consists of those things *you don't know about yourself* and *others don't know about you*. This is where a relationship with God can shed a lot of light. Why? Because God knows you better than you know yourself. If you want to discover who you are, you need to seek God. It's in seeking God that we discover our true identity in Christ. If you're going to maximize your potential, you've got to be in relationship with the God who gave you that potential in the first place!

This is also where we need the help of the Holy Spirit. When I went through my forgiveness exercise, I was a little shocked at how many grudges I was holding, how many offenses I had taken. The Holy Spirit was gracious enough to convict and to comfort. And it's not one or the other. It's got to be both/and. If you don't listen to *everything* the Spirit has to say, you won't hear *anything* the Spirit has to say. Why? It's a package deal. If you harden your heart to the voice of conviction, you won't hear the voice of comfort.

What is the loudest voice in your life? Is it the still, small voice of the Spirit? If it is, you'll say sorry more than the average person! You'll also forgive more than the average person. Why? You're living unoffended, loving unoffended.

Is there anyone you need to forgive?

What are you waiting for?

Part 3

THE THEOLOGY
OF *THANKS*

There are lots of ways to say thanks.

Thanks.
Thanks a lot.
Thanks a million.
Thank you kindly.
I can't thank you enough.

My personal favorite? *Thanks a latte.* Actually, I use the word *grateful* more than *thankful.* Why? Research has shown that it's even more effective at conveying gratitude. According to one therapist, being thankful is a *feeling,* while being grateful is an *action.*[1] Either way, the theology of *thanks* begins with gratitude.

Our family has four core values: gratitude, generosity, humility, and courage. Those four values overlap, but gratitude is the engine room. Gratitude is giving credit where credit is due. It's a fundamental recognition that every good and perfect gift comes from God.[2] In the words of theologian and former prime minister of the Netherlands Abraham Kuyper, "There is not a square inch in the whole domain of our human existence over which Christ, who is Sovereign over *all,* does not cry: 'Mine!' "[3] It's all *from* God and it's all *for* God.

"There are only two ways to live your life," said Albert Einstein. "One is as if nothing is a miracle. The other is as if everything is." I know people who say they've never experienced a miracle. With all due respect, you've never not.

Did you know that there are thirty-seven sextillion chemical reactions happening in the human body at any given moment?[4] The retina has 100 million neurons[5] that conduct close to ten billion calculations every second, and that's before an image even travels from the optic nerve to the visual cortex. With every heartbeat, six quarts of blood course their way through sixty thousand miles of veins, arteries, and capillaries. And don't forget DNA. If your genetic code, which is absolutely unique, were stretched end to end, it would measure twice the diameter of the solar system.

Are you sure you've never experienced a miracle?

Please! Sorry—I couldn't resist. Thanks for indulging me!

The English author and philosopher G. K. Chesterton wrote about the importance of taking nothing for granted—not a single sunrise, not a single smile, not a single second. "The idea of taking things with gratitude, and not taking things for granted," was what he called "the chief idea of my life."[6]

Are you taking things for granted?

Or are you taking things with gratitude?

"Grown up people are not strong enough to exult in monotony," said Chesterton. He also wrote, "It is possible that God says every morning, 'Do it again' to the sun; and every evening, 'Do it again' to the moon. . . . The repetition in Nature may not be a mere recurrence; it may be a theatrical *encore*."[7]

What if we approached each day as an encore? That's what

it is, isn't it? It never has been before and it never will be again. Gratitude is living each day like it's the first day and last day of your life!

The French poet Jacques Réda had a habit of walking the streets of Paris with the intention of seeing something new each day. That's how he renewed his appreciation for the city he loved.[8] Without that kind of intentionality, we become blind to the blessings all around us. The technical term is *inattentional blindness*. It's failing to see what's right in front of us.

Elizabeth Barrett Browning wrote,

Earth's crammed with heaven,
And every common bush afire with God:
But only he who sees, takes off his shoes,
The rest sit round it, and pluck blackberries.[9]

Are you taking off your shoes?

Or are you sitting around and plucking blackberries?

An old aphorism says, *Stop and smell the roses.* The saying traces back to Walter Hagen, a professional golfer who won eleven majors: "Don't worry—don't hurry. . . . Be sure to smell the flowers!"[10] That aphorism is an exhortation to slow down and savor life. Simply put, enjoy the journey! Jesus said it this way: "Consider the lilies."[11]

Many years ago, an exchange student from India attended our church. He had never seen snow, so when overnight flurries were forecast, he set his alarm clock for three in the morning. Why? He didn't want to miss the miracle! When I heard about it, I chuckled. Then I felt convicted. I had completely ignored what he thoroughly enjoyed.

Remember the axiom *Beauty is in the eye of the beholder*? It's true of everything.

When was the last time you made snow angels in freshly fallen snow? Or savored a sunset as an act of worship? Or marveled over a sleeping baby for a few minutes? Or stared into the night sky? Or enjoyed the laugh of a loved one?

11
Take a Breath

With every breath,
you literally inhale the history of the world.
—Jacket copy for *Caesar's Last Breath* by Sam Kean

Take a breath.

We don't give breathing much thought, unless we're choking or drowning or hiking at high altitudes. The average person inhales and exhales every four seconds. That adds up to 21,600 breaths every day. Over the course of our lives, most of us will tally 607,478,400 breaths. But who's counting?

Few things are more mundane than breathing, yet few things are more miraculous. With every breath, we inhale half a liter of air, which contains 12.5 sextillion molecules.[1] That's more molecules than all the sand on all the seashores on planet Earth, including sandcastles.

Take another breath.

The surface area of your lungs, with all their nooks and crannies, is the same size as a tennis court.[2] And all the airways—from your trachea to your bronchial tubes—measure 1,500 miles. "All the world's roads and all the world's canals and all the world's airports in the history of humankind," said Sam

Kean in his book *Caesar's Last Breath*, "haven't handled nearly as much traffic as our lungs do every second."[3]

With every breath, we inhale a complex combination of molecules. Oxygen, of course, is the most celebrated. You can't live more than a few minutes without it. And once you inhale it, red blood cells are ready and waiting like Amazon Prime to deliver those life-giving atoms. Speaking of, Amazon has a fleet of forty thousand trucks, thirty thousand vans, seventy airplanes, and who knows how many drones.[4] That's awfully impressive, especially the drones, but it pales in comparison with the average person. You have 25 trillion red blood cells, and each of those red blood cells contains 260 million hemoglobin proteins,[5] which deliver oxygen atoms on time, every time, all the time.

As we exhale, it may seem like our breath vanishes into thin air, but the molecules that make it up still exist. Under normal conditions, the air that we exhale catches prevailing winds and circles the globe at the same latitude in about two weeks. According to Kean, "Within about two months, the breath would cover the entire Northern Hemisphere. And within a year or two, the entire globe."[6]

In *Caesar's Last Breath*, Kean riffs on respiration and reframes the way we see the air around us. "With every breath, you literally inhale the history of the world. On the ides of March, 44 BC, Julius Caesar died of stab wounds on the Senate floor, but the story of his last breath is still unfolding; in fact, you're probably inhaling some of it now. Of the *sextillions* of molecules entering or leaving your lungs at this moment, some might well bear traces of Cleopatra's perfumes."[7]

Take one more breath.

Fill your lungs, like you're about to blow up a birthday balloon. Can you feel your lungs expand to full capacity? The history we inhale may be invisible, but the physiological effect is visceral. A deep breath calms your nerves and focuses your attention. It relieves stress and alleviates pain. It resets your mental state and recalibrates your emotional state. A deep breath is a signal to the rest of your body that you're safe.

Respiration is controlled by our autonomic nervous system. Breathing happens automatically, even when we're sound asleep, which is awfully amazing. But you can flip the switch from automatic to manual control with one deep breath.

The autonomic nervous system has parallel divisions. The sympathetic system is responsible for the fight-or-flight reflex. It functions like a fire alarm, and it activates adrenaline. The parasympathetic system does the exact opposite. It induces rest and relaxation, like spa music and scent diffusers. It pumps feel-good hormones like serotonin and oxytocin to the rest of the body.

Now juxtapose that with this.

Most of the nerves that are wired to the sympathetic system are located in the upper half of the lungs. When we take shallow breaths, it stimulates the fight-or-flight reflex. Most of the nerves that are wired to the parasympathetic system are located in the lower half of the lungs. To activate rest and relaxation, you have to breathe deeply. And it works whether you're shooting a free throw, defusing an intense argument, or meditating on Scripture. A deep breath recalibrates body, soul, and spirit.

Let everything that has breath praise the LORD.[8]

That is the last verse in the last psalm, and I love it for lots of reasons. If you're still breathing, God isn't finished with you yet. It's never too late to become who you might have been. This verse is also an open-ended invitation to worship. We don't need lyrics on a screen or a band onstage. All we need is breath— it's all the reason we need to praise God.

Fun footnote?

In Hebrew, the name of God is Yahweh. It was considered too sacred to say out loud, so the vowels were removed. All that's left are consonants: YHWH. According to some scholars, YHWH is the sound of breathing. On one hand, the name is too sacred to pronounce. On the other hand, it's whispered with every breath we take. It's our first word, last word, and every word in between.

Part of my fascination with respiration comes from the fact that I had asthma for forty years. After I prayed a bold prayer, one I had prayed hundreds of times before, God healed my lungs on July 2, 2016. I haven't touched an inhaler from that day to this day! I don't take a single breath for granted, but let me share one lesson I learned along the way: *Praise God for partial miracles.*

In the Gospels, there is a two-part miracle that is both fascinating and encouraging.[9] Jesus laid hands on a blind man, and the man experienced a miracle. His sight was restored, but not completely. People still looked like trees walking. Let's call it 20/100 vision. This is where many of us doubt God instead of praising Him for a partial miracle. This is where many of us give up because we didn't get the whole miracle. Listen—even Jesus had to pray twice! Some miracles happen in stages. These are the moments when we need to double down with prayer and fasting. All too often, we withhold our praise for partial miracles and then wonder why the whole miracle never happens. Why not praise God every step of the way, even if it's two steps forward and one step back?

On July 2, 2016, I prayed a bold prayer, and God completely healed my lungs. But the backstory involves a partial miracle. A month before that, I hiked Cadillac Mountain in Maine. It's certainly not the tallest mountain I've hiked, but I did so without the help of my inhaler. For me, that was huge! In fact, I went four days without using my inhaler, which was the longest such streak in my life at that point. I actually wondered whether the Lord had healed my asthma then, but I had to take my rescue inhaler on day five.

Having to take my inhaler knocked the wind out of me, pun intended. But instead of focusing on the fact that I had to take it again, I decided to praise God that I went four days without needing it. I actually praised God for that partial miracle publicly at a prayer night. It was less than a week later that He healed my asthma! Coincidence? I think not. Praising God for the partial miracle was a small step but a giant leap toward the double blessing of two healed lungs!

When you praise God for partial miracles, you are prophesying your praise! Gratitude is praising God *after* He does the miracle. Faith is praising God *before* He does. It's like a down payment on a miracle. Thank God before it happens; then see what happens! That *thanks* might just have a domino effect.

Is there a partial miracle you need to praise God for?

Take a deep breath.

Now pray a bold prayer!

12
Daily Reintroduction

I am every age, up to my own.
—MORRIE SCHWARTZ, IN *Tuesdays with Morrie*

Wilson Bentley took his first photomicrograph of a snowflake on January 15, 1885. "Under the microscope, I found that snowflakes were miracles of beauty," he said. "Every crystal was a masterpiece of design and no one design was ever repeated."[1] Bentley was right—no two snowflakes are the same. Scientists estimate as many as 10^{158} snowflake possibilities. That's 10^{70} times more varieties than there are atoms in the universe![2]

Wilson Bentley's curriculum vitae included 5,381 photographs of snowflakes, 2,300 of which were published in his magnum opus, *Snow Crystals*. And his holy curiosity never waned. In fact, he died the way he lived. He contracted pneumonia after walking six miles through a snowstorm and died on December 23, 1931. What a way to go! Doing what you love.

According to linguist Lucien Schneider, the Inuit dialect of Canada's Nunavik region has at least a dozen words for snow.[3] Why? They have a nuanced appreciation for and understanding of the different kinds of snow! On that note, linguistic research-ers have found a negativity bias in languages around the world: "There are more synonyms for a bad concept like pain than for its opposite, pleasure."[4] Therein lies the challenge.

Our gratitude is too generic! We celebrate snow when we could be celebrating every crystal in every snowflake. Am I tak-ing it too far? I think not. That is how an Orthodox Jew pro-nounces one hundred blessings per day.

They say a blessing *before* a meal and *after* a meal. They thank God for different ingredients, not just the main dish. And they celebrate aromas and tastes too. The more nuanced your *thanks* is, the more powerful it is. When it comes to *please, sorry,* and *thanks,* specificity is the silver bullet.

What if we did that with food? Instead of thanking God for Reese's Peanut Butter Cups, thank Him for chocolate *and* pea-nut butter. What an amazing combination! While you're at it, tip your cap to H. B. Reese, who invented those peanut butter cups in 1928. By the way, he had sixteen children, who I'm sure helped their father test the candy!

"No man steps into the same river twice," said the Greek philosopher, Heraclitus, "for it's not the same river and he's not the same man." That's true of everything isn't it? One secret to *thanks* is savoring things the second time. It's the difference be-tween joy and rejoicing. That's what the angels do!

> Bravo, GOD, bravo! . . .
> All angels shout, "Encore!"[5]

Nikola Tesla is one of history's most prodigious inventors. Tesla was granted more than a hundred U.S. patents. His most famous invention—the alternating-current power system—supplies our homes with easy access to electrical power. Every time you flip a switch, you owe Tesla a *thanks*.

Tesla is reported to have had a ritual that is both revealing and inspiring. During thunderstorms, he would sit on a couch near a window in his home. Every time lightning struck and thunder clapped, Tesla would rise to his feet and applaud God. It was one genius giving a standing ovation to another Genius.

For the record, there are approximately two thousand thunderstorms on planet Earth at any given time. And lightning strikes about forty times per second—3.46 million times per day! That is a lot of standing ovations, but according to the psalmist, the angels shout "Encore" after each one!

When was the last time you clapped for the Creator? When was the last time you gave Him a standing ovation? When was the last time you thanked God for a baby's smile or a child's laugh or your spouse's touch? When was the last time you were so awed by the night sky or autumn leaves or snowcapped mountains or ocean waves that you worshipped the Creator in wide-eyed wonder?

"Worship is transcendent wonder," said the Scottish essayist Thomas Carlyle. "Wonder for which there is now no limit or measure."[6] Picture a man who has lived his entire life in a cave, then steps outside for the first time and witnesses the sunrise. That caveman would watch with rapt astonishment the sight we daily witness with indifference!

The theology of *thanks* starts with the things we take for granted. It's cultivating profound gratitude for the things we overlook and underappreciate. The sunrise ranks right up there!

At this very moment, Earth is spinning on its axis at one thousand miles per hour, yet somehow you maintain your balance. Our planet is speeding through space at sixty-seven thousand miles per hour, and you don't even get dizzy. If that isn't a miracle, I'm not sure what is! Even on a day when you didn't get much done, you did travel 1.6 million miles through space. So there's that.

When was the last time you thanked God for keeping us in orbit? When was the last time you knelt at the end of the day and said, "Lord, I wasn't sure we were going to make the full rotation today, but You did it again." We don't pray that way. Why? Because God is so good at what God does that we take it for granted. The angels shout "Encore," and maybe we should too!

"The secret to love—and a sense of joy and gratitude toward all of life," wrote M. J. Ryan, "is to see, feel, and hear as if for the First Time. Before the scales of the habitual clouded the brilliant blue sky outside your office window, the tangy juiciness of an orange, or the softness of your loved one's hands. Before you got so used to her kind words, his musical laughter, that they became invisible."[7]

May you fall in love all over again! With what? With everything. With everyone.

As John O'Donohue said, "Relationships suffer immense numbing through the mechanism of familiarization."[8] The Nobel laureate Gabriel García Márquez once said about his wife, Mercedes, "I now know her so well that I haven't the slightest idea what she is really like."[9]

According to one study, the average married couple spends twenty-seven minutes in meaningful conversation.[10] No, not per day. Per week! The last time I checked, we change every day! That change may not be measurable, but I'm not who I was yesterday. And neither are you. "Every day we change as individuals based on our experiences that day," said Scott and Jill Bolinder. "In order to build a growing relationship as a couple, then, we must make time to 'daily reintroduce' ourselves to each other."[11] That idea of daily reintroduction is powerful, and it applies to a thousand things.

Just a few weeks after their miraculous deliverance from Egypt, the Israelites started complaining about the manna. If I remember correctly, manna was a miracle. The Israelites were literally complaining about a *miracle*! Unbelievable, right? Not so fast. We fall into the same trap. Isn't marriage miraculous? Children? The human body? The human mind? I bet you've filed a few complaints about each of those.

The Israelites said, "We remember the fish we ate freely in Egypt and without cost, the cucumbers, melons, leeks, onions, and garlic."[12] Seriously? It was free because *you weren't*. Israel's problem—our problem—is selective memory.

The bottom line? We don't see the world as it is. We see the world as we are. If you're looking for something to complain about, you'll always find it. If you're looking for something to give thanks for, you'll always find it. And your words—be they words of complaint or gratitude—will create your interior world.

Is there anything you're taking for granted?

Are there any miracles you're complaining about?

Is there something you need to applaud God for?

Pull a Tesla, and give God a standing ovation!

13

The Attitude of Gratitude

The more I considered Christianity,
the more I found that while it had established a rule
and order, the chief aim of that order was to give
room for good things to run wild.
—G. K. CHESTERTON, *Orthodoxy*

In 1942, an Austrian psychiatrist named Viktor Frankl was arrested by the Nazis. He would spend three years in four different concentration camps, including Auschwitz. Frankl was stripped of his possessions, his clothes, even his name. He was reduced to a number—prisoner 119,104. His mother and father, as well as his wife, would die in those concentration camps.

The year after his liberation, Viktor Frankl wrote a book titled *Man's Search for Meaning*. A survey conducted for the Library of Congress ranked it as one of the thirteen most influential books in the United States.[1] In that book, Frankl shared the secret to his survival. He said, "Everything can be taken from a man but one thing: the last of the human freedoms—to choose one's attitude in any given set of circumstances."[2]

In psychology, mental health is measured on a spectrum from depression to flourishing. Flourishing is evidenced by optimism, empathy, and authenticity. It's inner joy. It's self-esteem. It's a strong sense of purpose. On the other side of the spectrum is depression. It's evidenced by hopelessness and helplessness. It's feeling like the best is behind you.

Between depression and flourishing, there is languishing, "the neglected middle child of mental health." It's not mental illness, but it's not mental wholeness. It's apathy instead of empathy. It's no-man's-land. It's feeling blah. It's a lack of focus, lack of motivation, lack of vision.[3]

When it comes to languishing, there are lots of causes. Let me focus on two of them. One is loneliness, and the other is purposelessness. Remember when Elijah defeated the 450 prophets of Baal? You would think he would have been on cloud nine, but he found himself in a deep depression. In all fairness, he was receiving death threats from Queen Jezebel. So there's that. When someone is trying to kill you, it tends to affect your mental health! But there is another factor that is easily overlooked: "He went on alone into the wilderness."[4]

Did you catch it? Not only was Elijah in the wilderness; he was also all alone! We have never been more connected, technologically speaking. And we've never been more disconnected. Why? Digital doesn't do it. In fact, the distance created by digital devices can cause us to demonize one another. There, I said it.

"He who has a *why* to live for," said Friedrich Nietzsche, "can bear almost any *how*."[5] In the same sense, we can bear almost any burden if we have the right people in our corner. After the

Exodus, the Israelites found themselves fighting the Amalekites. Moses interceded for them, but his hands got heavy. That's when Aaron and Hur held up his arms, and as long as they did, Israel prevailed.[6] All of us need an Aaron and a Hur now and then, here and there. We need people who will lift us up when we're feeling down.

I recently rode my first bike century. Along with 180 other riders, I biked a hundred miles in a little under six hours. I felt great the first fifty miles. The last fifty? I had some doubts about whether my training was sufficient. With seven miles to go, I hit a hill and my quads started cramping. I had fallen behind the pack when the race organizer, Jeff Zaugg, dropped back to join me. He did more than give me a pep talk; he let me draft behind him up the hill. Jeff is six feet seven, so that's a pretty decent draft.

We all need to draft, don't we? We need someone to bear our burdens. We need someone to spur us on. We need someone to pick us up when we're ready to throw in the towel.

Take my life; I am no better than my ancestors.[7]

That is some stinking thinking! Elijah threw a pity party, and the problem was purposelessness. "Where there is no vision, the people perish."[8] The word *perish* refers to fruit that is rotting. Vision is a preservative. It will keep you young! The best way to stop sinning isn't to stop sinning. That'll work for a week or two. You need a vision that is bigger and better than the temptation you face!

Carl Jung believed that seemingly insurmountable problems can't be solved; they can only be outgrown![9] We have to discover something more important than the problem. In other words, we need a purpose that redeems our pain. When we find our purpose, the problem loses its power and goes away!

When the Israelites were enslaved by the Egyptians, their lives were made miserable by cruel taskmasters. They were so discouraged they couldn't be encouraged. And it's hard to blame them. When all you've ever known is slavery, it's hard to imagine anything else. Despite the promise of deliverance, the Israelites were despondent.

They did not listen to Moses, because of their broken spirit.[10]

One translation uses the phrase *anguish of spirit*.[11] You could easily add an *l—languish*. That phrase in Hebrew is *qotser ruach*, and it can be translated a few ways. It can mean "diminished spirit" or "shortness of breath." The Israelites were breathing shallow. Remember the sympathetic nervous system? The Israelites were constantly trying to catch their breath because of the backbreaking work. The phrase *qotser ruach* can also be translated "voicelessness." Without breath, you can't speak.

Are you languishing?

Or are you flourishing?

The tipping point, the turning point, is *thanks*! It's the difference between positivity and negativity. Once again, it was ten negative people who kept the Israelites out of the Promised Land. It was ten negative people who cost the Israelites forty years in the wilderness! Positivity isn't just a function of personality; it's a function of theology.

As I see it, we live at the intersection of two theologies, two realities. The *faithfulness* of God is pursuing us from the past—*so far, so God*. "Surely goodness and mercy shall follow me all the days of my life."[12] And the *sovereignty* of God is setting us up for the future—*the best is yet to come.* We are God's workmanship, created in Christ Jesus to do good works, which God has prepared in advance.[13] Simply put, God's got this. God's got you.

What is the locus of your confidence? Is it your education? Your résumé? Your bank account? Or is it the promises of God? The character of God—His goodness, His faithfulness? Truth be told, my self-confidence is below average. But my holy confidence is off the charts. I've seen too many miracles to not believe God for the next one! Don't tell me He can't do it—and by *it,* I mean anything! Positivity is standing on the promises of God.

Doubt is letting your circumstances get between you and God. I'm certainly not suggesting that you ignore reality. You need to confront the brutal facts, but you need to do so with unwavering faith.[14] Faith is putting God between you and your circumstances.

If you want to move from languishing to flourishing, there are no easy answers. And there are no quick fixes. But this I know for sure: You won't get there without gratitude. You can't control your circumstances, but you can control your response. Gratitude is the difference between bitter and better.

J. I. Packer earned his doctor of philosophy from Oxford University and served as general editor of the English Standard Version. He wrote more than fifty books including the all-time classic *Knowing God.* And he taught theology at Regent College in Vancouver, Canada, for almost four decades. I share his curriculum vitae because it helps pack this punch. "The purpose of theology," said J. I. Packer, "is doxology." Full stop.

Packer started every class by singing the doxology. Theology is the study of God, but the goal isn't knowledge. "Knowledge puffs up."[15] The goal is worship! Whatever you don't turn into praise turns into pride. Whatever you don't turn into praise turns into pain. Theology that doesn't lead to doxology is spiritual constipation. Most of us are educated way beyond the level of our obedience already. We don't need to know more; we need to do more with what we know! Or maybe I should say, we need to worship more with what we know!

In his brilliantly titled book, *Mozart's Brain and the Fighter Pilot*, Richard Restak shared a profound truism: *Learn more, see more.* "The richer my knowledge of the flora and fauna of the woods," wrote Restak, "the more I'll be able to see." He went on to say, "Our perceptions take on richness and depth as a result of all the things that we learn. . . . What the eye sees is determined by what the brain has learned."[16]

When astronomers look into the night sky, they have a greater appreciation for the constellations. They see more because they know more. When musicians listen to a symphony, they have a greater appreciation for the chords. They hear more because they know more. When sommeliers sample wine, they have a greater appreciation for the texture. They taste more because they know more.

On a recent trip to Florida, the volume and variety of trees sparked my curiosity. So I downloaded an app that enabled me to identify them. Technology is amazing, isn't it? Lora indulged me the rest of our trip as I said, "Guess what kind of tree that is?" By the way, banyan trees may be my new favorite! Beyond beautiful.

Learn more, see more.

Did you know that whale songs travel up to ten thousand miles underwater? Call me Ishmael, but that's amazing! And they aren't the only underwater songsters. Ichthyologists have discovered that some species of fish sing together at dawn and at dusk.[17] And it may not qualify as singing, but octopuses are the masters of camouflage. They also have three hearts and nine brains![18] Sorry—I geek out on this stuff. If you haven't seen the Academy Award–winning documentary *My Octopus Teacher,* do yourself a favor and watch it.

Can we have a little more fun?

The male wood thrush can harmonize by singing two notes using both sides of his Y-shaped voice box.[19] The brown thrasher has more than two thousand songs in its repertoire.[20] And after a six-thousand-mile migration, the male bobolink sings a three-and-a-half-second song to delineate territory and woo a mate.[21]

> I heard every creature in heaven and on earth and under the earth and in the sea. They sang:
>
> "Blessing and honor and glory and power
>   belong to the one sitting on the throne
>   and to the Lamb for ever and ever."[22]

Did you notice the four dimensions? The song of creation is four-dimensional—in heaven, on earth, under the earth, and in the sea. We may not be able to hear it, but it's happening nonetheless. And I'm not just talking about Beyoncé riding radio waves.

Every atom in the universe sings. According to Arnold Sommerfeld, a German physicist and pianist, a single hydrogen atom emits more frequencies than a grand piano. With its eighty-eight keys, a grand piano can produce eighty-eight frequencies. A hydrogen atom emits one hundred frequencies.

In his book *A Cup of Coffee at the Soul Cafe,* Leonard Sweet wrote that a carbon atom produces the same harmonic scale as a Gregorian chant. Things that make you go "Hmmmmm"! "Could it be that all carbon-based life," said Sweet, "is actually built on the Gregorian chant?"[23]

When I was a freshman in college, I took a class in immunology at the University of Chicago Hospital Center. It still ranks as my favorite class in undergrad. It made me want to be a doctor—for a semester. Of course, that would have entailed med school. I opted for a doctor of ministry degree instead.

I'm not sure whether my professor believed in intelligent design, but every class felt like an exegesis of Psalm 139:14: "I am fearfully and wonderfully made." I remember walking away from a lecture one day praising God for hemoglobin. Yes, hemoglobin. That class gave me a profound appreciation for the complexities of the human body. It also conceived in me a conviction that *every ology is a branch of theology.* Every square inch of creation reveals a unique dimension of God's personality and creativity.[24]

As A. W. Tozer said, "Eternity will not be long enough to learn all He is, or to praise Him for all He has done."[25] If Tozer is right, what are we waiting for? Just as delayed obedience is disobedience, delayed gratitude is ingratitude. God deserves our praise every second of every minute of every hour of every day!

I recently read a book by A. J. Jacobs titled *Thanks a Thousand.* He decided to thank every person who made his morning cup of coffee possible. And no, he didn't just mean the barista who pulls shots or makes French press coffee. There is quite a supply chain behind every cup of coffee, which starts with coffee farmers but also includes truck drivers, warehouse supervisors, forklift operators, and coffee roasters. Jacobs ended up thanking at least 964 people![26] Of course, there were some people he couldn't thank. Like the Ethiopian goatherd who discovered coffee beans in the first place.

I have to admit, that gratitude project got me thinking. Every *thanks* has a genealogy, and when you understand the backstory of the blessing, saying thanks becomes even more enjoyable. Your *thanks* takes on new dimensions, new authenticity. And like the Mandelbrot set, it's infinitely complex.

Gratitude is the gift that keeps on giving! Like fine wine, good memories get better with age. Sometimes a single *thank you* isn't sufficient.

What if we made it our mission to thank every person who has directly or indirectly affected our lives in a positive way? I know—it would take the rest of our lives to do so! And some people might be hard to track down, like the doctor and nurses who welcomed you into the world. But why not pick a few people and say thanks?

Many years ago, I had dinner with former NFL MVP Brett Favre. He was awfully down to earth, so I wasn't surprised by his Hall of Fame speech. He spoke for a record thirty-six minutes, and by my count, he said thanks no less than thirty-five times! He thanked his family. He thanked his coaches and teammates. He thanked the fans. He thanked the coach who recruited him in college. He even thanked the best man in his wedding!

Who has left their fingerprints on your soul? Who believed in you when nobody else did? Who was there through thick and thin? Make a list. Track them down, if you can. And say thanks!

I recently had a conversation with my high school basketball coach, Bob Sterr. It had been two decades since I had last talked to him. You know what I remember most? After I graduated from high school, he came to see me play in college! I'll never forget that, and I wanted him to know. He went out of his way, and it did more than make my day. Saying thanks closed the loop—it was a full-circle moment.

I can't promise that gratitude will cure whatever ails you, but it's a good place to start. Gratitude isn't getting what you want; it's appreciating what you have. And it can reduce stress, resolve conflict, and reverse aging. According to Dr. Bill Malarkey, professor emeritus of endocrinology at Ohio State University, "Stress is the single greatest determinant of aging. The antidote to stress is gratefulness." Maybe Ponce de León was looking in the wrong place! The fountain of youth isn't a place. It's the attitude of gratitude.

Who do you need to thank?

What are you waiting for?

14

Flip the Blessing

No one has ever become poor from giving!
—ANNE FRANK, "Give"

A few decades ago, Cornell University did a study with a self-explanatory title—"Sweetening the Till: The Use of Candy to Increase Restaurant Tipping."[1] Customers who are given a piece of candy along with their check tip more than those who don't get candy! I'm not sure a study was necessary to draw that conclusion, but generosity begets generosity.

Remember John Bargh and the idea of priming? We don't just prime with our words; we prime with our actions. It's the law of reciprocity. When someone receives something, they feel compelled to return the favor in kind. This is hardwired into the human soul.

Many years ago, someone came into my office and handed me a gift. Yes, please! I was a little confused, however, because it wasn't my birthday and it wasn't a holiday. My puzzled expression prompted an explanation: "Wise men come bearing gifts." File that under "things that make you go 'Hmmmmm.'" It's hard to argue with, isn't it?

I live by a little mantra: *Flip the blessing*. I wrote a book about it, *Double Blessing,* but here is the CliffsNotes version: We are blessed in order to bless. What God does for us is never just for us; it's always for others. God doesn't bless us to raise our standard of living; He blesses us to raise our standard of giving.

Whenever someone blesses me, I take careful inventory. But I don't just count the blessing. I try to return the favor by flipping the blessing for someone else. That's how gratitude grows. If you give me a car, I'm not going to sell mine and pocket the cash. I'm going to give my car away too. Why? Why not! I love receiving, but it's not nearly as fun as giving.

In 1996, we were planting a church in Washington, D.C. We started out in a D.C. public school, but about nine months into our launch, we landed in the movie theater at Union Station. We needed to purchase lights to do church in the movie theater, but we didn't have any spare cash sitting around. At the time, our church income was $2,000 a month, and we needed $5,000 to purchase the light kit. I'll never forget getting a $5,000 gift from a church in Hampton, Virginia. That gift changed the trajectory of our church.

Since that time, NCC has given more than $25 million to kingdom causes. We've given large gifts and small gifts, but the most meaningful gifts are $5,000. That's how we flip the blessing. That's how we say thanks.

When Lora and I were newly married, barely making ends meet, I was preaching at a church in the Chicago area. After the message, an older gentleman came up to shake my hand, but this was no ordinary handshake. There was a twenty-dollar bill hidden in his hand. He slipped it into mine and said, "Take your wife out to lunch." It's not one of the largest, but it is one of the most meaningful honorariums I've ever received. He called it a Pentecostal handshake.

Over the years, I've tried to flip that blessing in my own unique way. Sometimes it's a straight-up Pentecostal handshake, like the one I received. Sometimes it's leaving a tip that is larger than the bill. Sometimes it's dropping two-dollar bills for kids to find. That might sound like poor stewardship, but I take my inspiration from Boaz. He instructed his harvesters to intentionally drop some of the barley for Ruth to find.[2]

What does any of that have to do with *thanks*? If you live a life of gratitude, what goes around comes around. Your generosity will eventually catch up with you. It's the law of measures— "Give, and it will be given to you"[3]—which is synonymous with the law of reciprocity. You can't break the law of measures; it will make or break you. You get out of it what you put into it. And by *it*, I mean anything! Simply put, sow what you want to see more of.

It's true: You have not because you ask not. But if all you ever do is ask, your *please* rings hollow. The most effective way to ask is to give! "Giving a gift can open doors," said King Solomon. "It gives access to important people!"[4]

In his book *Giftology*, John Ruhlin talked about helping a group who was trying to get an interview with a Target executive. For eighteen months they had tried every angle but with no success. Ruhlin did a little research and discovered that the executive was a graduate of the University of Minnesota. He said, "We then hired a custom furniture company to have the Minnesota Gopher logo and fight song carved into a fifty-inch long, sixty-pound piece of cherry wood."[5] Within twenty-four hours, the executive's assistant called and set up a meeting!

Make sure you check your motives! If your creativity outpaces your authenticity, it might be manipulation. If your motives are selfish, it will come back to bite you. If you're trying to add value, no strings attached? Doors will fly open faster than you can say "Open sesame"! Once you say thanks, let the chips fall where they may. Your *thanks* will be only as effective as it is authentic.

Can I offer a few exhortations at this juncture?

1. *Don't accumulate possessions; accumulate experiences.* I've met only a few people possessed by a demon, but I've met lots of people possessed by their possessions. They don't own things; things own them!
2. *Raise your standard of giving.* We make a living by what we get, but we make a life by what we give. One of the defining moments in our journey of generosity was the day we stopped setting getting goals and started setting giving goals. It shifted our focus from how much we could make to how much we could give.
3. *You can't outgive God.* I don't believe in the prosperity gospel. Anytime you add an adjective to the gospel, you actually subtract from it. You can't play God like a slot machine. Besides, the greatest return on investment isn't monetary. It's joy unspeakable and the peace that passes understanding. You can't put a price tag on those things!

About a decade ago, Lora and I made a decision to personally gift a copy of every book I write to every person who attends National Community Church. We give away thousands of books before we sell a single copy. If you have a scarcity mentality, it may seem like we're losing sales. We don't see it that way. An abundance mindset recognizes that the more you give, the more God can bless! That's not name it, claim it. That's the law of measures.

There is a second law of equal importance—the law of treasures.

> Do not store up for yourselves treasures on earth, where moth and rust destroy, and where thieves break in and steal. But store up for yourselves treasures in heaven, where moth and rust do not destroy, and where thieves do not break in and steal. For where your treasure is, there your heart will be also.[6]

God doesn't need your money! He owns the cattle on a thousand hills, and He owns the hills. He doesn't need your money, but He wants your heart, and those two things are inextricably linked. Money issues are heart issues. Just as your face tells your body how to feel, your money tells your heart what to value.

We live in a culture that measures success by how much you make and how many people work for you. In the kingdom, success is measured by how much you give and how many people you serve.

If you want to flip the blessing, you have to be really good at gratitude! "A man embezzles from God," says the Talmud, "when he makes use of this world without uttering a blessing."[7]

There is a running debate among linguists: "Do words *reflect* a psychological state or do they *cause* it?"[8] In case you haven't figured it out by now, I fall into the second camp. Words don't just create worlds; they create our psychological state. A simple thanks can shift your outlook and shift the atmosphere.

When I say the word *worship,* many of us associate that with singing songs from a screen in a corporate church setting. When we worship that way, we are mirroring what is happening in heaven. But it's only one dimension of worship. For me, the truest form of worship—the purest form—isn't singing lyrics someone else has written. It's worshipping God with my own words in my own way! That's why I keep a gratitude journal. That's how I capture my thoughts and make them obedient to Christ. For me, *thanks* is a spiritual discipline.

My gratitude journal is the way I give thanks in all circumstances.[9] It's the way I enter His courts with thanksgiving.[10] It's the way I acknowledge that every good and perfect gift comes from above.[11] It's the way I give God the sacrifice of praise.[12] It's the way I sing a new song to the Lord.[13]

My first job was working at a gas station making minimum wage. One of my responsibilities was taking inventory. If I didn't inventory what we sold, it didn't get restocked. In much the same way, keeping a gratitude journal is the way we take inventory of our blessings. Then, and only then, can we flip the blessing.

It's worth repeating: Words create worlds. Joy isn't getting what you want. It's appreciating what you have! In the words of Kenton Beshore, "I want what I have."[14] It might be worth saying that every day!

Giving thanks isn't just looking backward. It's also looking forward with holy anticipation. How did Jesus endure the cross? By focusing on "the joy that was set before him." In the same way, we need to fix our eyes on Jesus, "the author and finisher of our faith."[15]

Dr. Emily Balcetis has done some fascinating research involving Olympic athletes and peak performance. When people focused on the finish line, it felt 30 percent closer. Those who focused on the finish line increased their pace by 23 percent and expended 17 percent less effort.[16] Simply put, your focus determines your reality!

The best way to fix your focus is to count your blessings. Once you do, flip those blessings for others! Your external circumstances may not change, but your internal attitude will. So will your *thanks*! Why? It will be filled with gratitude.

In the science of hermeneutics, there is a concept called the interpretive horizon. It's what's established when we read the opening sentence of a book. "Call me Ishmael," the opening line of Herman Melville's *Moby-Dick,* may be the most famous. I'd rank *A Tale of Two Cities* by Charles Dickens right up there. "It was the best of times, it was the worst of times." The opening line gives us a place to stand. It gives us a glimpse of what's possible. Of course, nothing compares with Genesis 1:1: "In the beginning God created the heavens and the earth."

Thanks is the genesis and revelation of God's blessing. It expands our interpretive horizon on all of life. Giving thanks to God and to others is the way gratitude goes full circle. But it also creates a virtuous cycle. Ingratitude stops the flow of blessing. Why? We are blessed to bless! When we give thanks, when we flip the blessing, we become a conduit of God's blessing.

When our kids were young, I came across this snippet titled "Introduction to Property Law from a Toddler's Perspective."

If I like it, it's mine.
If I can take it away from you, it's mine.
If it looks like mine, it's mine.

If I saw it first, it's mine.
If you're having fun with it, it's mine.
If you lay it down, it's mine.
If it's broken, it's yours.

According to the Talmud, there are four types of people characterized by these four mindsets:

1. What's yours is mine.
2. What's yours is yours.
3. What's mine is mine.
4. What's mine is yours.

The first person is a *taker*—what's yours is mine. The second and third persons are *matchers*—what's yours is yours and what's mine is mine. The fourth person is a *giver*—what's mine is yours. This person, according to the Talmud, is a *saint*.[17]

Which one are you?

Are you a taker?

Are you a matcher?

Or are you a giver?

Remember the little boy who gave his brown-bag lunch—five loaves and two fish—to Jesus? When you put what you have in your hands into God's hands, five plus two doesn't equal seven anymore! It doesn't add up; it multiplies: $5 + 2 = 5,000$ R12. There was more left over than He started with. How is that even possible?

Most of us, in a similar situation, would have complained about our lack. Am I right? Jesus didn't do that, did He?

Looking up to heaven, he gave thanks.[18]

What did He do? He gave thanks!

Don't let what you don't have keep you from praising God for what you do have. In the same vein, don't let what you can't do keep you from doing what you can. Most of us think we'd be more grateful, more generous, if we had more. I love you, but I'm not buying what you're selling. Gratitude starts right here, right now.

Count the blessing.

Flip the blessing.

Rinse and repeat.

15

The Overview Effect

You have never talked to a mere mortal.
—C. S. LEWIS, "The Weight of Glory"

In December 1968, *Apollo 8* **escaped Earth's orbit** and circled the moon ten times. It was a monumental mission, setting the stage for a lunar landing the following year. On Christmas Eve, astronaut Bill Anders saw Earth coming up over the horizon, so he grabbed his Hasselblad camera and started clicking. The aim of the mission was to identify potential landing sites on the moon, the only reason they had a high-resolution camera onboard. Anders used that camera to capture an iconic image: *Earthrise.*

That picture was worth more than a thousand words!

Like looking in a mirror, it gave us a glimpse of planet Earth in all its glory. The poet Archibald MacLeish described it this way on Christmas Day 1968: "To see the earth as it truly is, small and blue and beautiful in that eternal silence where it floats, is to see ourselves as riders on the earth together."[1]

When astronauts leave Earth's atmosphere and get a glimpse of our planet, it's almost like an out-of-body experience. It's called the overview effect. The view from outer space changes inner space! Psychologists have studied the overview effect, analyzing interviews, surveys, and autobiographies from more than a hundred astronauts and cosmonauts. Adam Grant summarized their findings: "Upon returning from space, astronauts are less focused on individual achievements and personal happiness, and more concerned about the collective good."[2] *Apollo 14* astronaut Edgar Mitchell put it this way: "You develop an instant global consciousness . . . an intense dissatisfaction with the state of the world, and a compulsion to do something about it."[3]

The overview effect is all about seeing the big picture. We share common ground with every person on the planet. And, I might add, common grace. It's a paradigm shift that puts our planet into perspective.

Are we focused on our differences, which are many?

Or are we focused on our common identity as image bearers?

A shift in focus can make all the difference in the world. It can even bridge the gap between fans of rival teams. In his book *Think Again*, Adam Grant gave one example:

In one experiment, psychologists randomly assigned Manchester United soccer fans a short writing task. Then they staged an emergency in which a passing runner slipped and fell, screaming in pain as he held his ankle. He was wearing the T-shirt of their biggest rival, and the question was whether they would stop to help him. If the soccer fans had just written about why they loved their team, only 30 percent helped. If they had written about what they had in common with other soccer fans, 70 percent helped.[4]

Remember Daniel Kahneman? People are endlessly complicated and interesting! That's a good starting point, but let me push the envelope. Everyone is invaluable and irreplaceable. The Talmud says it this way: "Whoever destroys a single life is considered by Scripture to have destroyed the whole world, and whoever saves a single life is considered by Scripture to have saved the whole world."[5]

"There are no *ordinary* people," said C. S. Lewis. "You have never talked to a mere mortal. . . . It is immortals whom we joke with, work with, marry, snub, and exploit."[6] There is a transitive property in Scripture that governs the way we treat people. We show hospitality as if we were entertaining angels.[7] We serve others as if they were Jesus Himself.[8]

Lewis included this addendum: "This does not mean that we are to be perpetually solemn. We must play. But our merriment must be of that kind . . . which exists between people who have, from the outset, taken each other seriously—no flippancy, no superiority, no presumption."[9]

As we've seen, blessing is God's most ancient instinct. It's also our deepest longing. The fourth-century church father Augustine of Hippo prayed, "Our heart is restless until it rests in you."[10] The French philosopher Blaise Pascal wrote that there is a God-shaped hole in every heart.[11] Pope Francis spoke about nostalgia for God.[12] Whatever label you choose, it's the image of God in us. We were made *by* God and *for* God.

Every piece of clothing has a label that reveals where it was made—Made in Canada, Made in Mexico, Made in America. If you had a label, it would say, Made in the image of God. You are God's workmanship, and the theology of *thanks* starts and stops there.

What we seek is something called shalom—it's the only

thing that will fill that God-shaped hole in the human heart. Or maybe I should say, shalom is the by-product of God filling our hearts. *Shalom* is the Hebrew word for "peace," and it was a standard greeting that conveyed a wish for health, wealth, and prosperity. Of course, we have a tendency to reduce complex theological concepts to clichés, so let me widen the aperture. Shalom is the restoration of all things to their original intent. It's the Garden of Eden before the Fall. It's a dimension of reality that the Bible calls heaven, a dimension we'll experience fully after the curse is reversed.

We tend to think of peace as emotional equilibrium, and I don't want to discount that internal dimension. Shalom is peace that passes understanding. It's peace in the midst of the storm. But peace is more than an emotion; peace is a person!

Remember the iconic moment when Jesus stopped a storm on the Sea of Galilee? He rebuked the wind and said to the waves, "Peace, be still."[13] Who does that? I'll tell you who—the Prince of Peace!

At its core, shalom is relational harmony, and it consists of four dimensions:

1. Right relationship with God
2. Right relationship with self
3. Right relationship with others
4. Right relationship with creation

The first dimension is right relationship with God, which is true north. The first tenet of the Westminster Catechism says that "man's chief end is to glorify God, and to enjoy him forever."[14] We get the glorifying God part, but the enjoying part is harder to grasp. John Piper called it Christian hedonism, which sounds like a misnomer. It's the conviction that God's ultimate goal and our deepest desire are one and the same thing! "God is most glorified in us," said Piper, "when we are most satisfied in Him."[15]

How much are you enjoying your relationship with God? That's not easy to measure, but it's an accurate indicator of spiritual maturity. To grow in relationship with God is to enjoy His Word, enjoy His presence. It's to enjoy everything that helps us draw near to Him.

The key to that right relationship is His righteousness. "God made him who had no sin"—Jesus—"to be sin for us, so that in him we might become the righteousness of God."[16] *Religion* is spelled *do*—it's all about what you can do for God. *Christianity* is spelled *done*—it's all about what Christ accomplished on the cross for you.

When our vertical relationship with God is out of whack, it results in idolatry issues. We seek lesser gods and settle for fifteen minutes of fame. We play the blame game and the shame game. An idol is anything you love more, trust more, or desire more than God. As John Calvin aptly stated, "Man's nature . . . is a perpetual factory of idols."[17]

Those idols cause complications in all four quadrants of shalom. "The low view of God . . . is the cause of a hundred lesser evils," said A. W. Tozer. "The man who comes to a right belief about God is relieved of ten thousand temporal problems."[18]

The second dimension of shalom is right relationship with self. We'll call this dimension due south. This is where idolatry issues turn into identity issues. If we find our identity in idols, we're building a house of cards. Instead of resting in the righteousness of Christ, we try to save ourselves via self-righteousness. It's the gospel of good works, which leaves the Cross out of the equation.

I have a theory of identity that might seem counterintuitive, but it's true. The more you have going for you, the more potential you have for identity issues. Why? It's easier to find your identity in something outside your relationship with God. There is nothing wrong with the degrees you've earned, the money you've made, or the physique you've worked hard for. But the second you find your identity or your security in those things, you've crossed a line. That goes for spiritual gifts too. God gave you those gifts, but you'd better use them for His glory, not yours. Otherwise those idols turn into false identities and false securities.

The third dimension of shalom is right relationship with others. The image of God in me greets the image of God in you. This is where a theology of dignity comes from. There never has been and never will be anyone like you. That isn't a testament to you. It's a testament to the God who created you. The significance of that is this: No one can worship God like you or for you. No one can take your place!

Most of us will never see the inside of a jail cell, but we're prisoners of one or two or three experiences in our past. We let the Enemy blackmail us. And to make matters worse, we project our pain onto others, which results in a compound fracture.

I love a good book title, and Louie Giglio wrote a recent favorite: *Don't Give the Enemy a Seat at Your Table.* What does that mean? Here's my take. If you harbor unforgiveness in your heart, you're giving the Enemy a seat at your table. If you hold a grudge or gossip behind someone's back, you're giving the Enemy a seat at your table. If you take offense, you're giving the Enemy a seat at your table. If you let fear dictate your deci-sions, you're giving the Enemy a seat at your table. Here's one more that may be less apparent. If you fail to give thanks, you're giving the Enemy a seat at your table.

The bottom line? Your sin is forgiven and forgotten. If you have nothing else to be thankful for, you still have the Cross! You still have the empty tomb. Your future is as bright as the promises of God. When the Enemy reminds you of your past, remind him of his future!

The fourth dimension of shalom is right relationship with creation, and there are two mistakes we need to avoid. The first is worshipping created things. The second is abusing the cre-ation we're called to care for. We need to be great at the Great Commission. Jesus's last command needs to be our first con-cern, but let's not forget our Genesis commission:

> Be fruitful and multiply. Fill the earth and govern it. Reign over the fish in the sea, the birds in the sky, and all the ani-mals that scurry along the ground.[19]

How do we govern the earth? For starters, we enjoy it. I love God's reaction to His creation: "God saw that it was good."[20] That simple refrain appears five times in the creation narrative. Then on the sixth day, almost like someone experiencing the overview effect, God stepped back and surveyed the full scope of His creation: "God saw all that he had made, and it was very good."[21] God was awed by His own creation!

When was the last time you stepped back and enjoyed a sun-rise?

When was the last time you looked up at the stars?

When was the last time you celebrated the goodness of God in a simple smile?

Remember the ten lepers that Jesus healed? All ten were healed of their physical ailment, but only one of them was healed of something much worse—ingratitude. It was that one leper who doubled back to Jesus, fell at His feet, and said thanks![22]

I think many assume that Adam and Eve would have remained in the Garden of Eden forever if they hadn't eaten from the tree of the knowledge of good and evil, but that is a misreading of the text. God invited Adam and Eve to explore. Everything outside Eden was uncharted territory. They could travel 24,901 miles in any direction and never see the same landscape twice. There were 196,949,970 square miles of virgin territory to explore. We glorify God by exploring, learning about, and enjoying everything He created. And, of course, by taking care of it for future generations!

The astronomer who charts the stars, the geneticist who maps the human genome, the researcher who seeks a cure for Parkinson's disease, the oceanographer who explores the Great Barrier Reef, the ornithologist who preserves rare bird species, the physicist who tries to catch quarks, the chemist who studies molecular structures—all of them have one thing in common. All of them are explorers. They are fulfilling the Genesis commission. And their explorations honor God if they're done for the right reasons and result in the right response: knowing God and making Him known.

Shalom is right relationship with God, self, others, and creation. That relational harmony is modeled by the Trinity. We believe in one God who is three persons. The Trinity is three-part harmony. The early church fathers called it perichoresis. It's a choreographed dance between Father, Son, and Holy Spirit. The Trinity is shalom in motion.

What does that have to do with *please, sorry,* and *thanks?*

Those three magic words sing in three-part harmony. A pretty *please* opens hearts and minds and doors. A simple *sorry* can mend broken relationships. A heartfelt *thanks* is the flywheel of gratitude. Get good at them, and life becomes a choreographed dance filled with love and joy and peace.

According to Cornelius Plantinga, "Sin is *culpable* disturbance of shalom."[23] If that is true—and I think it is—then *please, sorry,* and *thanks* are the way shalom is restored. It's the way we hit the reset button. On that note, let's go back to the beginning.

If you want to change your life, you have to change your words.

Words create worlds!

Why not start with *please, sorry,* and *thanks?*

Notes

Introduction

1. Kary Oberbrunner, *Unhackable: Close the Gap Between Dreaming and Doing* (Powell, Ohio: Ethos Collective, 2020), 12.

2. Steve Cohen, *Win the Crowd: Unlock the Secrets of Influence, Charisma, and Showmanship* (New York: Collins, 2006), 135.

3. Abraham Joshua Heschel, quoted in Susannah Heschel, introduction to *Moral Grandeur and Spiritual Audacity,* by Abraham Joshua Heschel, ed. Susannah Heschel (New York: Farrar, Straus and Giroux, 1997), viii.

4. Eugene T. Gendlin, *Focusing* (New York: Bantam Books, 2007), 3–4.

5. Deepika Choube and Shubham Sharma, "Psychological and Physiological Effect in Plant Growth and Health by Using Positive and Negative Words," *International Journal of Innovative Research in Technology* 8, no. 1 (June 2021), www.ijirt.org/master/publishedpaper/IJIRT151445 _PAPER.pdf.

6. Proverbs 18:21.

7. Hayim Nahman Bialik and Yehoshua Hana Ravnitzky, eds., *The Book of Legends—Sefer Ha-Aggadah: Legends from the Talmud and Midrash,* trans. William G. Braude (New York: Schocken Books, 1992), 704.

8. James 3:9.

9. James 3:4.

10. Matthew 12:34, BSB.

11. Eva Van Prooyen, "This One Thing Is the Biggest Predictor of Divorce," The Gottman Institute, www.gottman.com/blog/this-one-thing-is-the-biggest-predictor-of-divorce.

12. Genesis 1:3.

13. Leonard Bernstein (speech, American International Music Fund, May 21, 1963), www.loc.gov/resource/musbernstein.100020111.0/?sp=1&r=-0.14,0.176,1.247,0.819,0.

14. John 1:1–3.

15. Drake Baer, "15 Olde English Words We Need to Start Using Again," *Business Insider,* May 5, 2016, www.businessinsider.com/olde-english-words-we-need-to-start-using-again-2016-4.

16. Susie Dent, in Nickee De Leon Huld, "How Many Words Does the Average Person Know?," *Word Counter* (blog), https://wordcounter.io/blog/how-many-words-does-the-average-person-know.

17. Dale Carnegie, *How to Win Friends and Influence People,* rev. ed. (New York: Gallery Books, 2022), xx.

Part 1: The Psychology of *Please*

1. *APA Dictionary of Psychology,* s.v. "word-association test," https://dictionary.apa.org/word-association-tests.

2. Valeria Sabater, "Carl Jung's Word Association Test," Exploring Your Mind, November 15, 2021, https://exploringyourmind.com/carl-jung-word-association-test.

3. John A. Bargh, Mark Chen, and Lara Burrows, "Automaticity of Social Behavior: Direct Effects of Trait Construct and Stereotype Activation on Action," *Journal of Personality and Social Psychology* 71, no. 2 (1996): 233–35.

4. "The 'Magic Words,'" The Emily Post Institute Inc., https://emilypost.com/advice/the-magic-words.

5. "The 'Magic Words,'" The Emily Post Institute Inc.

6. Ajai Prakash, "Christian Herter Was the Governor of . . . ,"
    Sermon Central, February 21, 2008, www.sermoncentral
    .com/sermon-illustrations/65172/christian-herter-was-the
    -governor-of-by-ajai-prakash.

7. Philippians 2:3–7, BSB.

8. Matthew 7:12, NASB.

1: There *You* Are

1. Jennie Jerome, quoted in Robert Mening, "A Story from
    a Dinner Party Winston Churchill's Mother Attended
    Over a Century Ago Illustrates What It Means to Be a
    Charismatic Leader," October 27, 2016, *Business Insider,*
    www.businessinsider.com/charismatic-leadership-tips
    -from-history-2016-10.

2. Benjamin Disraeli, quoted in Dale Carnegie, *How to Win
    Friends and Influence People,* rev. ed. (New York: Gallery
    Books, 2022), 116.

3. Francis Schaeffer, in "The Virtue of Listening—Because
    There Are No Little People . . . ," The Humanitas Forum
    on Christianity and Culture, February 3, 2015, https://
    humanitas.org/?p=3229.

4. Edith Schaeffer, in "The Virtue of Listening."

5. "Theodore Roosevelt's Libraries," Theodore Roosevelt
    Center, Dickinson State University, www.theodore
    rooseveltcenter.org/Learn-About-TR/TR-Encyclopedia
    /Reading-and-Writing/Roosevelt-Libraries.aspx.

6. Adam Grant, *Give and Take: A Revolutionary Approach to
    Success* (New York: Viking, 2013).

7. Jim Elliot, *The Journals of Jim Elliot,* ed. Elisabeth Elliot
    (Grand Rapids, Mich.: Revell, 2002), 174.

8. Matthew 25:40.

9. James W. Pennebaker, *The Secret Life of Pronouns: What Our
    Words Say About Us* (New York: Bloomsbury, 2011), ix.

10. Grant, *Give and Take,* 36.

11.   Grant, *Give and Take*, 36.

12.   James W. Pennebaker, quoted in Jessica Wapner, "He Counts Your Words (Even Those Pronouns)," *New York Times*, October 13, 2008, www.nytimes.com/2008/10/14/science/14prof.html.

13.   Rabbi Jonathan Sacks, *Not in God's Name: Confronting Religious Violence* (New York: Schocken, 2015), 51.

14.   Cindy K. Chung and James W. Pennebaker, "The Psychological Functions of Function Words," ResearchGate, January 2007, www.researchgate.net/profile/Cindy-Chung-2/publication/237378690_The_Psychological_Functions_of_Function_Words/links/0a85e52f1898d247c2000000/The-Psychological-Functions-of-Function-Words.pdf.

15.   1 Samuel 14:35.

16.   1 Samuel 15:12, NLT.

17.   Daniel 3:1–6.

18.   1 Samuel 18:7.

19.   1 Samuel 18:8, NLT.

20.   1 Samuel 18:9, NLT.

21.   John Damascene, quoted in Thomas Aquinas, *Summa Theologiae*, part 2 of part 2, "Question 36. Envy," New Advent, www.newadvent.org/summa/3036.htm.

22.   Robert Madu (speech, WAFBEC, Iganmu, Nigeria, January 8, 2021), http://blog.wafbec.org/day-6-evening-session-1-pst-robert-madu.

23.   Stephen R. Covey, *The 7 Habits of Highly Effective People: Powerful Lessons in Personal Change* (New York: Free Press, 2004), 207.

2: Open Sesame

1.   Denzel Washington, quoted in Cheyenne Roundtree, "Denzel Washington Pays Tribute to Late Mentor and Friend Sidney Poitier: 'He Opened Doors for All of Us,'" Daily Beast, January 7, 2022, www.thedailybeast.com

/ denzel-washington-pays-tribute-to-late-mentor-and
-friend-sidney-poitier-he-opened-doors-for-all-of-us.

2.   Sidney Poitier, "Sidney Poitier Reflects on Lessons from
     Childhood," interview, ABC News, February 20, 1985,
     https:// abcnews.go.com/ Entertainment/ video/ sidney
     -poitier-reflects-lessons-childhood-82137840.

3.   Winn Collier, *A Burning in My Bones: The Authorized Biogra-*
     phy of Eugene H. Peterson (Colorado Springs, Colo.: Water-
     Brook, 2021), 155.

4.   Eugene H. Peterson, *Under the Unpredictable Plant: An Ex-*
     ploration in Vocational Holiness (Grand Rapids, Mich.: Eerd-
     mans, 1994), 50.

5.   Yvette Alt Miller, "Sidney Poitier and the Jewish Waiter
     Who Taught Him How to Read," Aish, January 11, 2022,
     www.aish.com/ ci/ a/ Sidney-Poitier-and-the-Jewish-Waiter
     -who-Taught-Him-How-to-Read.html.

6.   Sidney Poitier, quoted in "Sidney Poitier, First Black Actor
     to Win Best Actor Oscar, Dies at 94," *Globe and Mail,* Janu-
     ary 7, 2022, www.theglobeandmail.com/ arts/ film/ article
     -sidney-poitier-first-black-actor-to-win-best-actor-oscar
     -dies-at-94.

7.   Sidney Poitier, quoted in Patricia Bosworth, "Sidney
     Poitier on the Rough Road to Hollywood," *Washington*
     Post, May 25, 1980, www.washingtonpost.com/ archive
     /entertainment/ books/ 1980/ 05/ 25/ sidney-poitier-on-the
     -rough-road-to-hollywood/ 436a15fe-f67e-4b49-a83c
     -5cb7412a2e4a.

8.   William Osler, quoted in "In Memoriam—Sir William
     Osler," *Canadian Journal of Medicine and Surgery* 47, no. 3
     (March 1920): 116.

9.   Revelation 3:20, ESV.

10. Aesop, "The North Wind and the Sun," *The Aesop for Chil-*
     dren, Library of Congress, https:// read.gov/ aesop/ 143
     .html.

11. Ephesians 4:2.

12. Romans 2:4.

13. Selena Gomez, "Kill 'Em with Kindness," track 2 on *Revival*, Interscope Records, 2015.

14. Matthew 7:7.

15. Psalm 84:11, KJV.

16. Matthew 7:9–11.

17. James 4:2.

3: Say It with a Smile

1. Joey Reiman, *Thinking for a Living: Creating Ideas That Revitalize Your Business, Career & Life* (Athens, Ga.: Longstreet, 1998), 77–79.

2. Reiman, *Thinking for a Living*, 158–59.

3. "On Average a Woman Smiles 62 Times a Day; Men Smile Only 8 Times," South Florida Reporter, May 30, 2018, https://southfloridareporter.com/on-average-a-woman-smiles-62-times-a-day-men-smile-only-8-times.

4. Mark Stibich, "10 Big Benefits of Smiling" Verywell Mind, updated September 10, 2022, www.verywellmind.com/top-reasons-to-smile-every-day-2223755.

5. Stibich, "10 Big Benefits of Smiling."

6. Daniel 1:12, NLT.

7. Daniel 1:20.

8. Daniel Goleman, *Emotional Intelligence: Why It Can Matter More Than IQ* (New York: Bantam Books, 2020), 30.

9. Daniel 2:14.

10. Marilyn Chandler McEntyre, *Caring for Words in a Culture of Lies* (Grand Rapids, Mich.: Eerdmans, 2009), 54.

11. McEntyre, *Caring for Words*, 44.

12. McEntyre, *Caring for Words*, 45.

13. Mark 10:51.

14. Proverbs 15:23, NLT.

15. Proverbs 27:14, BSB.

16.   Emily Dickinson, "Tell All the Truth but Tell It Slant," in *Dickinson Poems,* ed. Peter Washington (New York: Alfred A. Knopf, 1993), 18.

4: Wash Feet

1.   James W. Pennebaker, *The Secret Life of Pronouns: What Our Words Say About Us* (New York: Bloomsbury, 2011), 61.

2.   Becky Upham, "Facebook Comes Under Fire After Whistleblower and Leaked Documents Reveal Negative Impact on Girls," Everyday Health, October 9, 2021, www.everydayhealth.com/public-health/facebook-comes-under-fire-after-whistleblower-and-leaked-documents-reveal-negative-impact-on-young-girls.

3.   Georgia Wells, Jeff Horwitz, and Deepa Seetharaman, "FaceBook Knows Instagram Is Toxic for Teen Girls, Company Documents Show," *Wall Street Journal,* September 14, 2021, www.wsj.com/articles/facebook-knows-instagram-is-toxic-for-teen-girls-company-documents-show-11631620739.

4.   Brooke Auxier, "64% of Americans Say Social Media Have a Mostly Negative Effect on the Way Things Are Going in the U.S. Today," Pew Research Center, October 15, 2020, www.pewresearch.org/fact-tank/2020/10/15/64-of-americans-say-social-media-have-a-mostly-negative-effect-on-the-way-things-are-going-in-the-u-s-today.

5.   Maria Pengue, "16 Eye-Opening Negative News Statistics You Need to Know," *Letter.ly,* March 29, 2021, https://letter.ly/negative-news-statistics.

6.   Pengue, "16 Eye-Opening Negative News Statistics."

7.   Ephesians 4:29, NLT.

8.   *Encyclopaedia Britannica,* s.v. "George Gerbner," www.britannica.com/biography/George-Gerbner.

9.   Angela Watercutter, "Doomscrolling Is Slowly Eroding

Your Mental Health," *Wired*, June 25, 2020, www.wired
.com/story/stop-doomscrolling.

10.   Genesis 4:9.

11.   C. S. Lewis, *The Screwtape Letters* (New York: HarperOne,
      2001), 162.

12.   Mark 15:15.

13.   Mark 15:14.

14.   John 9.

15.   "Diffusion of Innovation Theory," Boston University School
      of Public Health, September 9, 2019, https://sphweb
      .bumc.bu.edu/otlt/mph-modules/sb/behavioralchange
      theories/behavioralchangetheories4.html.

16.   John 13:3–4.

17.   Matthew 23:11.

18.   James 4:17.

5: Words Matter

1.   Sidney Greenberg, *Lessons for Living: Reflections on the
      Weekly Bible Readings and on the Festivals* (Bridgeport,
      Conn.: Hartmore House, 1985), 93.

2.   Brett Favre (speech, Pro Football Hall of Fame, Canton,
      Ohio, August 6, 2016), www.youtube.com/watch?v=xoKt
      _Q9xD0A.

3.   Numbers 12:1.

4.   Jeremiah 1:6.

5.   Jeremiah 1:7.

6.   Jeremiah 1:7.

7.   Matthew 5:37, BSB.

8.   Matthew 12:37.

9.   Scott Sauls, *A Gentle Answer: Our "Secret Weapon" in an Age
      of Us Against Them* (Nashville, Tenn: Nelson, 2020), 14.

10.   Ephesians 4:29, AMPC.

11. Genesis 27:38.

12. Genesis 27:38, ESV.

13. Genesis 1:28, NLT.

14. A. W. Tozer, *The Knowledge of the Holy: The Attributes of God, Their Meaning in the Christian Life* (San Francisco: HarperSanFrancisco, 1961), 1.

15. Zephaniah 3:17.

16. Matthew 3:17, KJV.

17. Matthew 10:12–13, NLT.

18. Bob Goff, *Everybody Always: Becoming Love in a World Full of Setbacks and Difficult People* (Nashville, Tenn.: Nelson Books, 2018).

19. Luke 7:39.

20. Mark 14:9.

21. Laurie Beth Jones, *Power of Positive Prophecy: Finding the Hidden Potential in Everyday Life* (New York: Hyperion, 1999), ix.

22. Randy Frazee, *His Mighty Strength: Walk Daily in the Same Power That Raised Jesus from the Dead* (Nashville, Tenn.: Nelson Books, 2021), 48.

23. Psalm 119:11, KJV.

24. 1 Timothy 4:4–5.

25. Hebrews 4:12.

26. 2 Timothy 3:16.

27. Jeremiah 1:12, ESV.

28. Isaiah 55:11, KJV.

29. Romans 10:17, KJV.

30. Romans 10:9, NASB.

Part 2: The Science of *Sorry*

1. Graham Greene, *The Power and the Glory* (New York: Penguin Books, 2015), 13–14.

2. Michael Lewis, *The Undoing Project: A Friendship That Changed Our Minds* (New York: W. W. Norton, 2016), 53.

3. Rolf Smith, *The Seven Levels of Change: The Guide to Innovation in the World's Largest Corporations* (Arlington, Tex.: Summit, 1997), 49.

4. Ralph Waldo Emerson, "August 26," *Everyday Emerson: A Year of Wisdom* (New York: St. Martin's, 2022), 64.

5. Dale Carnegie, *How to Win Friends and Influence People,* rev. ed. (New York: Gallery Books, 2022), 32.

6. Emerson, "January 14," *Everyday Emerson,* 14.

7. Mark 9:41.

8. Luke 23:34, ESV.

9. Rachel Hartigan, "The Epic COVID-19 Memorial on the National Mall, in One Stunning Photo," *National Geographic,* September 30, 2021, www.nationalgeographic .com / culture / article / epic-covid-19-memorial-national -mall-one-stunning-photo.

10. Carnegie, *How to Win Friends,* 184.

11. Tom Jacobs, "Reading Literary Fiction Can Make You Less Racist: New Research Finds a Compelling Narrative Can Help Us Sidestep Stereotypes," PacificStandard, June 14, 2017, https:// psmag.com/social-justice/reading-literary -fiction-can-make-less-racist-76155.

12. George Orwell, "Looking Back on the Spanish War," in *Facing Unpleasant Facts: Narrative Essays,* ed. George Packer (Boston: Mariner Books, 2009), 149.

13. Jonathan Glover, *Humanity: A Moral History of the Twentieth Century,* 2nd ed. (New Haven, Conn.: Yale University Press, 2012), chap. 11.

14. Matthew 18:22, NLT.

15. Lewis B. Smedes, *Forgive and Forget: Healing the Hurts We Don't Deserve* (San Francisco: HarperSanFrancisco, 1996), x.

9: Secret Sauce

1. Matthew 7:1.

2. Matthew 7:3–5.

3. Ice Cube, "Check Yo Self," track 13 on *The Predator,* UMG Recordings, 1992.

4. Frank Sesno, *Ask More: The Power of Questions to Open Doors, Uncover Solutions, and Spark Change* (New York: AMACOM, 2017), 1.

5. Sesno, *Ask More,* 58.

6. Sesno, *Ask More,* 74–76, 222; 91, 213–15; 158–60, 234.

7. *Tommy Boy,* directed by Peter Segal (Los Angeles: Paramount Pictures, 1995).

8. Roman Russo, "Remember the Losada Ratio of 2.9013 If You Want to Be Happy," Optimal Happiness, December 3, 2020, https://optimalhappiness.com/losada-ratio-losada -line-29013/#:~:text=Losada%20Ratio%20states%20that %20for,we%20are%20unhappy%20and%20languishing .com.

9. Hebrews 4:15.

10. Luke 4:1–13.

11. John 1:14.

12. Kim Scott, *Radical Candor: Be a Kick-Ass Boss Without Losing Your Humanity* (New York: St. Martin's, 2017), 9–10.

13. Scott, *Radical Candor,* 32.

14. John 8:7, NLT.

15. John 8:11, NLT.

16. John 11:21, 32.

17. John 11:43, KJV.

18. Matthew 22:37–39.

19. James 4:6.

20. Romans 8:1.

21.   Mike Foster, *People of the Second Chance: A Guide to Bringing Life-Saving Love to the World* (Colorado Springs, Colo.: WaterBrook, 2016), 7.

10: Unoffendable

1.   Corrie ten Boom, *Tramp for the Lord* (Fort Washington, Pa.: CLC, 2011), 55–57.

2.   Joshua 5:9, NLT.

3.   Bradford Veley, "Stuffed," https://bradveley.com/stuffed.

4.   1 Corinthians 2:9–10.

5.   "Stunning Details of Brain Connections Revealed," ScienceDaily, November 17, 2010, www.sciencedaily.com /releases/2010/11/101117121803.htm.

6.   Song of Songs 2:15.

7.   Matthew 11:30.

8.   Ephesians 4:30–32.

9.   R. T. Kendall, *Total Forgiveness: When Everything in You Wants to Hold a Grudge, Point a Finger, and Remember the Pain—God Wants You to Lay It All Aside*, rev. ed. (Lake Mary, Fla.: Charisma House, 2007), 6.

10.   Kendall, *Total Forgiveness*, 42.

11.   Proverbs 19:11.

12.   Acts 7:60.

13.   Huston Smith, *The World's Religions: Our Great Wisdom Traditions* (San Francisco: HarperSanFrancisco, 1991), 40.

Part 3: The Theology of *Thanks*

1.   Susan Rhoads, "The Difference Between Gratitude and Thankfulness," PMC, www.psychmc.com/articles /difference-between-gratitude-and-thankfulness.

2.   James 1:17.

3. Abraham Kuyper, quoted in Roger Henderson, "Kuyper's Inch," *Pro Rege* 36, no. 3 (March 2008): 12, https://digitalcollections.dordt.edu/cgi/viewcontent.cgi?article=1380&context=pro_rege.

4. Arsenio Rodriguez, "The Encounter: The Constant Motion of the Machinery of Life," *Feature*, May 2, 2021, www.meer.com/en/65608-the-encounter.

5. "Brain, Eyes and Computers: Peek at 1998 Moravec Book, Chapter 3," https://frc.ri.cmu.edu/~hpm/book97/ch3/retina.comment.html.

6. G. K. Chesterton, *The Autobiography of G. K. Chesterton* (San Francisco: Ignatius, 2006), 325.

7. G. K. Chesterton, *Orthodoxy* (Chicago: Moody, 2009), 92.

8. Phil Cousineau, *The Art of Pilgrimage: The Seeker's Guide to Making Travel Sacred* (Newburyport, Mass.: Conari, 2021).

9. Elizabeth Barrett Browning, "Aurora Leigh," in *Aurora Leigh, and Other Poems* (New York: James Miller, 1866), 265.

10. Walter Hagen, quoted in Grantland Rice, *The Tumult and the Shouting: My Life in Sport* (New York: A. S. Barnes, 1954), 73.

11. Matthew 6:28, ESV.

11: Take a Breath

1. Sam Kean, *Caesar's Last Breath: Decoding the Secrets of the Air Around Us* (New York: Back Bay Books, 2018), 75.

2. Kean, *Caesar's Last Breath*, 66.

3. Kean, *Caesar's Last Breath*, 9.

4. Walter Loeb, "How Amazon Could Speed Up by Dumping USPS," *Forbes*, May 12, 2022, www.forbes.com/sites/walterloeb/2022/05/12/amazon-may-replace-usps-as-a-delivery-agent/?sh=30c3c63562db.

5. Tatsuro Yoshida, Michael Prudent, and Angelo D'Alessandro, "Red Blood Cell Storage Lesion: Causes and

Potential Clinical Consequences," PMC, *Blood Transfusion* 17, no. 1 (January 2019): 27–52, www.ncbi.nlm.nih.gov /pmc/articles/PMC6343598.

6. Kean, *Caesar's Last Breath*, 9.

7. Kean, *Caesar's Last Breath*, book description, https:// samkean.com/books/caesars-last-breath.

8. Psalm 150:6.

9. Mark 8:22–25.

12: Daily Reintroduction

1. Wilson Bentley, quoted in "First Photograph of a Snowflake," Guinness World Records, www .guinnessworldrecords.com/world-records/606626-first -photograph-of-a-snowflake.

2. Alexis Stempien, "Are All Snowflakes Really Different? The Science of Winter," Smithsonian Science Education Center, December 16, 2015, https://ssec.si.edu/stemvisions -blog/are-all-snowflakes-really-different-science-winter.

3. "Inuktitut Words for Snow and Ice," *The Canadian Encyclopedia*, last modified December 14, 2017, www .thecanadianencyclopedia.ca/en/article/inuktitut-words -for-snow-and-ice.

4. John Tierney and Roy F. Baumeister, *The Power of Bad: And How to Overcome It* (London: Penguin Books, 2021), 8.

5. Psalm 29:1, MSG.

6. Thomas Carlyle, "The Hero as Divinity," in *Sartor Resartus, and On Heroes, Hero-Worship and the Heroic in History* (London: Macmillan, 1920), 265.

7. M. J. Ryan, *Attitudes of Gratitude: How to Give and Receive Joy Every Day of Your Life* (York Beach, Maine: Conari, 1999), 75–76.

8. John O'Donohue, *Anam Cara: A Book of Celtic Wisdom* (New York: Cliff Street Books, 1998), 90.

9. Plinio Apuleyo Mendoza and Gabriel García Márquez, *The Fragrance of Guava* (London: Verso, 1983), 23.

10. FamilyLife, "On Average, Married Couples Communicate Only 27 Minutes Per Week," Facebook, April 24, 2019, https://m.facebook.com/permalink.php?story_fbid= 10155923237231249&id=39717321248.

11. Scott Bolinder and Jill Bolinder, quoted in Les Parrott and Leslie Parrott, *Becoming Soul Mates: Cultivating Spiritual Intimacy in the Early Years of Marriage* (Grand Rapids, Mich.: Zondervan, 1995), 17.

12. Numbers 11:5, AMPC.

13: The Attitude of Gratitude

1. Esther B. Fein, "Influential Book," *New York Times*, November 20, 1991, www.nytimes.com/1991/11/20/books /book-notes-059091.html.

2. Viktor E. Frankl, *Man's Search for Meaning* (Boston: Beacon, 2014), 62.

3. Adam Grant, "There's a Name for the Blah You're Feeling: It's Called Languishing," *New York Times*, April 19, 2021, www.nytimes.com/2021/04/19/well/mind/covid -mental-health-languishing.html.

4. 1 Kings 19:4, NLT.

5. Friedrich Nietzsche, quoted in Frankl, *Man's Search for Meaning*, 97.

6. Exodus 17:8–16.

7. 1 Kings 19:4.

8. Proverbs 29:18, KJV.

9. C. G. Jung, *Commentary on "The Secret of the Golden Flower,"* in *Alchemical Studies*, trans. R. F. C. Hull (Princeton, N.J.: Princeton University Press, 1983), 15.

10. Exodus 6:9, ESV.

11. Exodus 6:9, KJV.

12. Psalm 23:6, ESV.

13. Ephesians 2:10.

14. Thanks to Jim Collins for his articulation of the Stockdale Paradox. See "The Stockdale Paradox," Jim Collins, www.jimcollins.com/concepts/Stockdale-Concept.html.

15. 1 Corinthians 8:1.

16. Richard Restak, *Mozart's Brain and the Fighter Pilot: Unleashing Your Brain's Potential* (New York: Three Rivers, 2001), 92.

17. Bec Crew, "Fish Have Been Recorded Singing a Dawn Chorus—Just like Birds," *ScienceAlert*, September 22, 2016, www.sciencealert.com/fish-have-been-recorded-singing-a-dawn-chorus-just-like-birds.

18. George Sranko, "Why Do Octopus Have 3 Hearts, 9 Brains, and Blue Blood? Smart Suckers!," *BioGeoPlanet*, https://biogeoplanet.com/why-do-octopuses-have-9-brains-8-arms-3-hearts-and-blue-blood-surprising-facts.

19. Joe Lowe, "Favorite Bird Sounds and Songs in the United States," American Bird Conservancy, April 6, 2019, https://abcbirds.org/blog/favorite-bird-sounds-songs-united-states.

20. Gareth Huw Davies, "Bird Songs," PBS, www.pbs.org/lifeofbirds/songs.

21. "Bobolink Range Map," All About Birds, www.allaboutbirds.org/guide/Bobolink/maps-range; "Bobolink Sounds," All About Birds, www.allaboutbirds.org/guide/Bobolink/sounds.

22. Revelation 5:13, NLT.

23. Leonard Sweet, *A Cup of Coffee at the Soul Cafe* (Nashville: Broadman & Holman, 1998), 65.

24. Romans 1:20.

25. A. W. Tozer, *The Pursuit of God* (Chicago: Moody, 2006), 47.

26. A. J. Jacobs, *Thanks a Thousand: A Gratitude Journey* (New York: TED Books, 2018), 109.

14: Flip the Blessing

1. David B. Strohmetz et al., "Sweetening the Till: The Use of Candy to Increase Restaurant Tipping," *Journal of Applied Social Psychology* 32, no. 2 (February 2002): 300–309, https://onlinelibrary.wiley.com/doi/abs/10.1111/j.1559 -1816.2002.tb00216.x.

2. Ruth 2:16.

3. Luke 6:38.

4. Proverbs 18:16, NLT.

5. John Ruhlin, *Giftology: The Art and Science of Using Gifts to Cut Through the Noise, Increase Referrals, and Strengthen Client Retention*, 2nd ed. (self-pub., 2018), 74.

6. Matthew 6:19–21, BSB.

7. Hayim Nahman Bialik and Yehoshua Hana Ravnitzky, eds., *The Book of Legends: Legends from the Talmud and Midrash*, trans. William G. Braude (New York: Schocken Books, 1992), 533:250.

8. James W. Pennebaker, *The Secret Life of Pronouns: What Our Words Say About Us* (New York: Bloomsbury, 2011), 14.

9. 1 Thessalonians 5:18.

10. Psalm 100:4.

11. James 1:17.

12. Hebrews 13:15.

13. Psalm 96:1.

14. Kenton Beshore, "Thanksgiving in Living" (sermon, Mariners Church, Irvine, Calif., November 22, 2020), www .youtube.com/watch?v=RmZUwUZv0qw.

15. Hebrews 12:2, KJV.

16. Emily Balcetis, "Why Some People Find Exercise Harder Than Others," TED, www.ted.com/talks/emily_balcetis _why_some_people_find_exercise_harder_than_others /transcript.

17. Pirke Avot 5:10, in *Pirke Avot: A Modern Commentary on Jewish Ethics,* trans. and ed. Leonard Kravitz and Kerry M. Olitzky (New York: UAHC, 1993), 82.

18. Matthew 14:19.

15: The Overview Effect

1. Archibald MacLeish, "A Reflection: Riders on Earth Together, Brothers in Eternal Cold," *New York Times,* December 25, 1968, www.nytimes.com/1968/12/25/archives/a-reflection-riders-on-earth-together-brothers-in-eternal-cold.html.

2. Adam Grant, *Think Again: The Power of Knowing What You Don't Know* (New York: Viking, 2021), 128.

3. Edgar Mitchell, quoted in Grant, *Think Again,* 128.

4. Grant, *Think Again,* 129.

5. Mishnah Sanhedrin 4:5; Yerushalmi Talmud 4:9.

6. C. S. Lewis, "The Weight of Glory," in *The Weight of Glory: And Other Addresses* (New York: HarperOne, 2001), 46.

7. Hebrews 13:2.

8. Matthew 25:40; Ephesians 6:7.

9. Lewis, "The Weight of Glory," 46.

10. Augustine, *Confessions,* trans. and ed. Henry Chadwick (Oxford: Oxford University Press, 2008), 3.

11. Blaise Pascal, *Pensées,* trans. A. J. Krailsheimer, rev. ed. (London: Penguin Books, 1995), 45.

12. Pope Francis, "Nostalgia for God" (message, *Domus Sanctae Marthae,* Vatican City, October 1, 2015), www.vatican.va/content/francesco/en/cotidie/2015/documents/papa-francesco-cotidie_20151001_nostalgia-for-god.html.

13. Mark 4:39, KJV.

14. The Westminster Shorter Catechism, 1647, www.westminsterconfession.org/resources/confessional-standards/the-westminster-shorter-catechism.

15. John Piper, *Desiring God: Meditations of a Christian Hedonist,* rev. ed. (Colorado Springs, Colo.: Multnomah Books, 2011), 288.

16. 2 Corinthians 5:21.

17. John Calvin, *Institutes of the Christian Religion,* ed. John T. MacNeill, trans. Ford Lewis Battles (Philadelphia: Westminster, 1960), 1:108.

18. A. W. Tozer, *The Knowledge of the Holy* (New York: Harper Collins, 1961), vii, 2.

19. Genesis 1:28, NLT.

20. Genesis 1:10, 12, 18, 21, 25.

21. Genesis 1:31.

22. Luke 17:11–19.

23. Cornelius Plantinga, Jr., *Not the Way It's Supposed to Be: A Breviary of Sin* (Grand Rapids, Mich.: Eerdmans, 1996), 18.

Delightful faith-filled picture books by
MARK BATTERSON and his daughter,
SUMMER BATTERSON DAILEY!

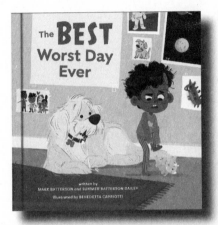

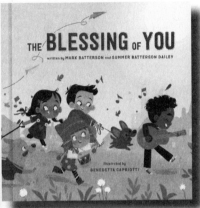

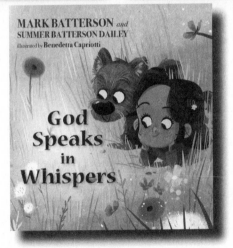

7 Daily Habits to Help You
Stress Less & Accomplish More

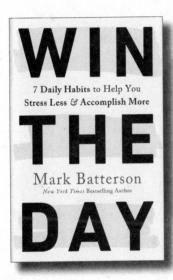

Turn the page on the past and seize the gift of today with seven practical yet life-changing habits.

Find free church resources, discussion questions, videos, and more at MarkBatterson.com/WinTheDay.

Unleash the power of twenty-four hours in your life and discover the quintessential catalyst for going after God-sized goals, one day at a time.

Learn more at MarkBatterson.com/DoItForADay.

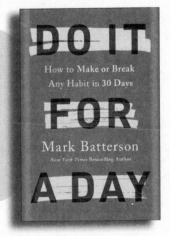